MAKE THEIR DAY!

EMPLOYEE RECOGNITION THAT WORKS

SIMPLE WAYS
TO BOOST
MORALE
PRODUCTIVITY
AND PROFITS

CINDY VENTRICE

BK

BERRETT-KOEHLER PUBLISHERS, INC.
San Francisco

Berrett-Koehler Publishers, Inc.
235 Montgomery Street, Suite 650
San Francisco, CA 94104-2916
Tel: (415) 288-0260
Fax: (415) 362-2512
www.bkconnection.com

Ordering Information
Quantity sales. Special discounts are available on quantity purchases by corporations, associations, and others. For details, contact the "Special Sales Department" at the Berrett-Koehler address above.
Individual sales. Berrett-Koehler publications are available through most bookstores. They can also be ordered direct from Berrett-Koehler: Tel: (800) 929-2929; Fax: (802) 864-7626; www.bkconnection.com
Orders for college textbook/course adoption use. Please contact Berrett-Koehler: Tel: (800) 929-2929; Fax: (802) 864-7626.
Orders by U.S. trade bookstores and wholesalers. Please contact Publishers Group West, 1700 Fourth Street, Berkeley, CA 94710. Tel: (510) 528-1444; Fax (510) 528-3444.

Berrett-Koehler and the BK logo are registered trademarks
of Berrett-Koehler Publishers, Inc.

Printed in the United States of America

Berrett-Koehler books are printed on long-lasting acid-free paper. When it is available, we choose paper that has been manufactured by environmentally responsible processes. These may include using trees grown in sustainable forests, incorporating recycled paper, minimizing chlorine in bleaching, or recycling the energy produced at the paper mill.

Library of Congress Cataloging-in-Publication Data

Ventrice, Cindy
   Make their day! : employee recognition that works / by Cindy Ventrice.
      p.   cm.
   Includes bibliographical references and index.
   ISBN 1–57675–197–X
      1. Incentive awards—United States.   2. Employee motivation—United States.
I. Title.
   HF5549.5.I5V336 2003
   658.3'142—dc21

                                                                      2002043710

         08 07 06 05 04 03   10 9 8 7 6 5 4 3 2 1

Interior Design & Typesetting by Desktop Miracles, Inc., Stowe, Vermont

contents

12-18-03

foreword

For the past quarter century, I've had one of the truly great jobs in journalism. My beat has been the workplace, specifically, great workplaces. It's been my lucky lot to visit and write about companies that employees rave about in a variety of books and magazine articles. For the past half-dozen years, I've worked with my fellow journalist Milton Moskowitz to identify and write about the "100 Best Companies to Work for in America" for *Fortune*.

These companies represent the spectrum of the business world and have ranged from extremely familiar names like Microsoft and FedEx to relative unknowns like TDIndustries and The Container Store. Regardless of the industry, size, age, or location of the companies, I've noticed that employees of these terrific workplaces invariably talk about how they feel treated as individuals, that they feel respected, that they feel the management recognizes their contributions to the organization.

As I've looked more closely at these companies, I've learned that it is no accident that employees feel so positively about their employers. Great workplaces are the result of the attitudes and actions of management. At the core, the management of these companies sincerely believes that the employees are the ones who are primarily responsible for the success (or failure) of the enterprise. As a result of this attitude, management sees the need to constantly recognize the value of the employees. They see positive recognition as part of their jobs, not as something that occurs once every five years when it is time to hand out the employee recognition awards.

Even in a bad workplace, it would not be surprising to find an individual manager who is good about showing appreciation toward employees. But how can this happen throughout an organization? This is precisely what *Make Their Day!* is all about—how to make employee recognition part of the fabric of an organization.

This is no ordinary management book, however. Cindy Ventrice has done her research. She's looked at a variety of companies and interviewed dozens of managers to look beneath the surface. There are many books on employee recognition, but this one is by far the best. Most books on this subject give examples of best practices in the field—in some cases hundreds of such examples. The idea seems to be that to improve employee recognition, managers should copy the policy or practice used by another organization.

The problem is that each company is unique. Each one has its own distinctive culture and history. What works in one company may completely backfire in another. But the approach of many managers simply ignores this seemingly obvious fact. Imitate what Company A does and you, too, will be successful.

That's where *Make Their Day!* can be so useful. Ventrice's book is full of lots of useful and provocative examples. But she goes beyond merely reciting cases. Using her in-depth interviews with managers at a variety of companies, Cindy Ventrice explores the deeper issues involved. She puts her finger on the all-important question of trust. How can you recognize people in such a way that trust is built? She points out that it is a question of relationships, not techniques. She shows that genuinely recognizing people means doing it all the time, not just on special occasions.

This book offers precisely the kind of insights that any manager interested in creating a great workplace should read.

Robert Levering

Robert Levering is coauthor of *Fortune*'s annual "100 Best Companies to Work for in America" and cofounder of Great Place to Work® Institute.

During nearly two decades as a business consultant, I've had the opportunity to observe a wide variety of workplaces in nearly every industry as well as many government and nonprofit agencies. Early on, when my consulting focused on helping companies make large-scale operational changes, I discovered that, when it comes to motivated employees, there is a whole spectrum of workplace possibilities. At one end of the spectrum is a workplace where people love to come to work. Employees are energetic, enthusiastic, and highly productive. At the other end, people seem to be going through the motions of their job, doing as little as possible, and hating every minute of it.

From the beginning, on my first visit into any company at the positive end of this spectrum, my immediate reaction was "Wow! This is a great place to work." When I first entered a workplace at the negative end, a more common reaction was "How quickly can I finish and get out of here?" Unfortunately for me, the less appealing the environment, the longer most projects took. People in these organizations were less cooperative, less communicative, and less willing to implement change. Time and time again, my experience proved to me, in a fairly dramatic manner, that a positive work environment means more productive employees.

Today I work with managers and employees on issues related to morale and motivation. I teach courses to help employees deal with burnout, increase their own job satisfaction, and become more productive. In the process, employees have taught me what their managers do, or neglect to do, that contributes to their becoming burned out. Much of what they describe qualifies, at some level, as lack of recognition. I also work with managers on a variety of issues related to job satisfaction. I teach them what employees tell me matters most and, in turn, learn what they do that receives the most positive response from employees. Most of what they describe qualifies in some way as recognition. Working with both employees and managers, one thing has become very clear. Recognition, in all its forms, strongly enhances morale and productivity.

Most organizations know that recognition is important. I estimate that every year U.S. companies spend about 18 billion dollars on recognition and incentives,[1] a little more than the combined annual revenue of Hasbro, Yahoo!, and Nike.[2] Eighty-six percent of organizations have some kind of recognition program in place,[3] and yet most employees still feel inadequately recognized. A national survey by Princeton-based management consulting firm Kepner-Tregoe showed that only 40 percent of workers feel adequately rewarded or recognized by their supervisor.[4] Why is it that, with all the money spent and all the programs in place, employees still don't feel recognized? It's simple, really: Employees want something different from what their organizations offer.

A few years ago I began asking employees from all over the country to tell me about recognition they had received that had a lasting impact and to describe what made that recognition memorable.[5] Many told me about recognition that had happened years earlier. They described organizations, managers, and coworkers to whom they felt a tremendous loyalty. They told me that recognition doesn't need to come from elaborate programs. They told me that the kind of recognition that motivates them to be and do their best is something else entirely.

The people who lead and manage some of the most exceptional workplaces in the nation understand how recognition affects motivation and use what they know to produce exceptional results. In preparing to write this book, I interviewed executives, managers, front-line supervisors, and the employees from some of these workplaces. Among those included in the book, you will find highly regarded companies such as Xilinx and Pella Windows and Doors, subsidiaries of high-profile companies such as Microsoft Great Plains Business Solutions and FedEx Freight, and companies well known only in their industries or geographical areas, such as Graniterock and Plante & Moran. I have also included a few companies that, as a whole, do an unremarkable job of motivating employees but have departments, supervisors, or individuals who are performing exceptionally. I have included organizations of all sizes that represent a variety of industries and geographical areas. What they all have in common are workplaces where employees feel a tremendous level of loyalty and work satisfaction and frequently outperform their counterparts in other departments or organizations.

The primary audience for this book is managers and supervisors, but this book is loaded with information that anyone can use. Human resource groups will get ideas on how they can administer more effective programs. Individuals can learn how to recognize their coworkers, their managers and supervisors, and even themselves! Senior executives can learn how to support their managers and administrators in creating more effective recognition.

The results of my observations and subsequent research are in this book. *Make Their Day!* will show you how to provide the kind of meaningful recognition people are looking for. You will learn about the variety of forms recognition can take, many of which managers rarely consider. You will learn about the simple ways you can recognize employees and boost motivation—regardless of how your organization views recognition or what external challenges you face. I invite you to continue reading and learn how you can make your job easier and create a more productive workplace using recognition that works.

CINDY VENTRICE
SANTA CRUZ, CALIFORNIA
MARCH 2003

acknowledgments

In writing this book, I had the help of literally hundreds of people whose stories and guidance helped deepen my understanding of what meaningful recognition really is. I want to express my appreciation to: my clients who, over the years, inspired my interest in the subject of recognition and allowed me to see firsthand how effective recognition could be; workshop participants who told me their tales from the workplace; survey respondents who provided the employees' perspective on recognition that works; and the numerous organizations that openly shared with me the successes—and even some of the failures—of their recognition practices. I am also grateful to the members of several on-line communities (Yahoo! Groups): ASTD-SV, TRDEV, and HRNET, who assisted me with my research. To all of these people, I say, "Thank you."

I am indebted to the many friends and colleagues who reviewed my manuscript and provided valuable feedback on both content and form as well as their own anecdotes on the subject of meaningful recognition.

Friend and fellow author Elizabeth Carlassare not only reviewed the manuscript but assembled a fantastic group of non-fiction writers who proved invaluable. Members of this group changed over time, and I am grateful to them all, but especially to Ben Hess, Joni Martin, Mignon Fogarty, Steve Balbo, Mark Marinovich, Patrick Letellier, Lydia Hanich, and Aimee McNamara for their commitment to this project. They offered moral support, diverse perspectives on my work, and some terrific editing!

Equally important were my colleagues—fellow members of ASTD (an organization dedicated to workplace learning and performance). They volunteered as reviewers, helped with title ideas, provided comments and suggestions, and asked probing questions that vastly improved the quality of my work. More people assisted me than I can possibly mention. Rest assured that I appreciate everyone's help and support. Special mention for going above and beyond goes to: Cindy Skrivanek, Patty Woolcock, Len Gomberg, Laura Browne, Michael Levick, Becky Baybrook, Pam Fontenot, Ben Bratt, Rebecca Linquist, Laura Gasewind, Paula Bailey, Debra Ward, Craig Harrison, Kari Ashe, and Diana Hartley.

I am also indebted to my friends and family for the moral support and gentle nudges that they provided. My husband and best friend, Gary, offered encouragement and kept things together while I completed this project. My son, Tony, who has always inspired me to take on new challenges, graciously allowed himself to be recruited as an editor. My close friend Mary Davis Marcum has been there for me every step of the way, patiently listening to me, providing important contacts, reading and editing numerous chapters, and learning far more about the subject of recognition than I am sure she ever wanted to know.

I also want to thank the business leaders and thought leaders who shared their views on recognition, read the manuscript, and provided their feedback and/or endorsement. These people include Rodger Stotz, Marshall Goldsmith, Sharon Jordan-Evans, Bill Catlette, Ken Blanchard, Millard Fuller, Michael Marcum, Kip Tindell, Norm Weiss, and Mike Little.

I especially want to thank Robert Levering, who is a leader in the effort to identify the great places to work. He generously shared his knowledge and research during the early stages of this book's development, read the completed manuscript, and agreed to write the foreword.

I am extremely grateful to my publisher, Steven Piersanti of Berrett-Koehler, and my editor, Jeevan Sivasubramaniam, for taking a chance on a new author and providing expert direction and guidance throughout the process. The entire Berrett-Koehler staff is a phenomenal group who pour their heart and soul into making each book a success. They all have my gratitude.

All my Berrett-Koehler reviewers were very helpful, offering suggestions that strengthened both content and structure. Special thanks goes to Kathleen Epperson, an independent organizational effectiveness consultant and Berrett-Koehler reviewer who read an article I had written, suggested that I contact them about writing a book, and started this whole adventure!

While my name is the one on the cover, this book has been a team effort. I am grateful to all those who generously offered their support and expertise to this project, from development to marketing. To each one, I say, "Thank you!"

Making Recognition a Priority

Make Their Day! is a book about *recognition that works*—recognition that is meaningful, memorable, and boosts morale, productivity, and profits. As you read this book you will learn simple, effective techniques that you can begin to implement today.

Many managers and supervisors will argue that they don't have time to make anyone's day; they're too busy making sure the work gets done. They are busy dealing with hiring freezes, layoffs, mergers and acquisitions, strikes, budget cuts, rising expenses, product defects, missed deadlines, or high turnover among in-demand workers. In terms of priorities, recognition typically comes dead last. While this may be understandable, it is a big mistake. Managing is easier when recognition is a priority.

Don't Put Recognition on Your To-Do List

After reading the heading for this section, you're probably thinking, "What do you mean, don't put recognition on your to-do list? If it's not on my to-do list, how can recognition be a priority? Isn't that a contradiction?" No, it isn't. I've seen many managers and supervisors who decided to make recognition a priority. They had the best intentions when they put "recognize employees" on to their to-do lists and then, as the weeks progressed and pressing matters demanded their attention, they slowly moved recognition farther and farther down the list. Even though their intentions were good, recognition never happened.

If you are a manager or supervisor, you probably have an overwhelming amount of responsibility. Even with the best intentions, if you add recognition to your oversized to-do list, there is a good chance that you won't get to it either. When you do manage to get to it, you're likely to do it once, check it off, and then forget about it. This isn't the kind of recognition that works.

Make Recognition the Header on Your To-Do List

Recognition isn't something you can do and then check off your list. You need to think of recognition a little differently. Instead of adding recognition to your to-do list, make it *the header*. Find ways to add recognition to every employee interaction. When you delegate, add a little praise of past accomplishments. When you receive project updates, thank employees for their promptness, thoroughness, or accuracy. When you hold a team meeting to talk about a new challenge, express confidence in the group's ability to meet that challenge. As you complete each item on your to-do list, think how you can incorporate recognition into it.

Make Your Job Easier!

Make recognition the header on your list, and you will find your job gets easier. There are hundreds of small things you can do to provide the recognition your employees crave without putting a greater strain on your time, things that positively affect the work environment because they provide the right kind of recognition. With the right recognition, you will find employees more willing to tackle problems on their own instead of bringing them to you to solve. With the right recognition, employees will show more concern about quality and reputation. With the right recognition, employees will be more willing to pitch in when things get difficult. Morale will go up. Absenteeism will go down. And your job will get easier.

One of the reasons many managers are overwhelmed is they're overseeing disgruntled, burned-out employees. While it is true managers can't control the outside factors that impact their departments, they can control how those factors affect the people who work for them. Managers can boost morale and, consequently, boost productivity and profits. Recognition that works does this—it energizes and revitalizes the workplace. It creates a loyal, motivated, and productive work force. And managing a loyal, motivated, and productive work force makes your job as a manager job easier.

Recognition That Works—*Works!*

Recognition that works—works!—even in the most challenging situations. To show you how, I want to take you inside Remedy

Support Services. In August 2001 Peregrine Systems purchased competitor Remedy Corporation, a software company that had more than twenty-five thousand employees and products in more than 60 percent of Fortune 1000 companies. While managers at Remedy were hopeful that the purchase would help them expand their operations and increase market share, they still faced typical merger issues: concerns about possible layoffs, culture changes, product direction, and the priorities of the parent company—challenges that many managers are very familiar with. During the next eight months, Peregrine Systems endured the same financial setbacks as most of the technology industry and suffered through the seemingly inevitable layoffs.[1]

This was only the beginning of the challenges that Remedy faced as part of Peregrine. Peregrine announced it had misstated revenue during the past two years, and the CEO and CFO resigned.[2] Remedy was restructured and 5 percent of the work force was laid off. Peregrine Systems stock continued a steady decline, class-action stockholder lawsuits accumulated, and by the time Remedy had been part of Peregrine Systems for ten months, Peregrine Systems stock had been delisted from NASDAQ.[3] Just over twelve months after it was acquired by Peregrine Systems, Remedy was sold to BMC Software.

Talk about a whirlwind of turmoil and change! Given the circumstances, it's easy to imagine employee morale would be at an all-time low. How could managers possibly keep employees productive under these conditions? Yet during the tumultuous ten month period from purchase to delisting, Remedy Support Service maintained employee morale and improved customer satisfaction ratings while continuing to grow their revenue stream![4]

Mike Little, VP of Worldwide Professional Services and Support, admits they never knew what was coming next. According to Little, they survived and even thrived because they set big goals for themselves, listened to employees, and showed their appreciation. As you will discover as you read this book, these three things are integral to offering meaningful and memorable recognition.

Visible Signs of Recognition

At Remedy Support Services, recognition that works takes many forms, some of which are very visible. Pirate ships constructed by each of Remedy's support groups offer a reminder of a friendly competition to be the best support team. Some managers give out stickers for perfect customer surveys, and employees display the stickers outside their cubicles. One employee was proud of a toy SUV his manager had presented him in recognition of his good work. Managers work hard to find fun and creative ways to improve performance and show employees they are valued.

Managers also hold Employee Appreciation Days where they wash employees' cars, prepare them food, play games, and dress up in costumes. According to employees, Employee Appreciation Days isn't an event the organization puts on, it's something the managers do for them. When I met with employees, they were getting ready to celebrate Employee Appreciation Days. Because of budget cutbacks, there was little discretionary money available. Many employees told me that instead of eliminating the celebration, managers chose to pay for it out of their own pockets. The gesture wasn't lost on the employees. It meant a lot to them.

Invisible Recognition

Remedy employees enjoy and respond well to the fun and games. But many companies try friendly competitions, prizes, and events with little or no success. These things only work because Remedy managers offer another kind of recognition as well—recognition that you might not even notice at first glance. Mike Little introduced me to many of the 100-plus employees in support services. During those introductions I discovered he knew everyone's name, how long they had been with the company, and where they had worked before. There is an easy camaraderie between Little and the unit's employees, and it exists because Little recognizes employee value by staying in touch with and caring about every individual.

Georgeann Beville, Director of Global Enterprise Support, says morale stays high because "we make sure employees know we are committed to them." One of the employees who reports to Beville said moral is high because "she understands what we are doing and supports us consistently." Beville's actions tell her people that she recognizes their value.

One of Remedy's tenets is "Hire the best and then trust them." There is a lot of recognition in that statement *if managers really believe it*. Remedy managers proved they meant it when Peregrine Systems required a second round of layoffs. These managers refused to follow outlined procedures. During the first round, they had followed protocol: personnel followed laid-off employees to their desks, waited while they packed up their belongings, and then escorted them out of the building. Following this first round of lay-offs, managers asked themselves, "Where is the trust in doing it this way?" They hated the message their actions sent.

During the second round, they handled it differently. They allowed employees to spend as much time as they liked packing up their things and saying their good-byes. No one followed them around, and no one restricted their access. Some employees finished quickly, and others spent the entire day. Several thanked their managers for allowing them to leave in this manner. The way the managers handled the layoff was a small gesture, but it meant a lot to employees—both those that stayed and those that left.

Managers at Remedy have built recognition into everything they do. It's the header on their to-do list and it makes all the difference to employees. It is the reason why, in the face of unbelievable turmoil, Remedy Support Services consistently improved customer satisfaction and increased revenue. As you read the chapters that follow, you will learn why the people in your workplace consider the kinds of recognition that Remedy offers so important.

Proven Techniques

Throughout this book you will learn about organizations that have demonstrated their ability to offer effective recognition. These organizations, as a whole, experience lower turnover and higher productivity and profitability than their industry averages. This point bears repeating: When employees give high ratings to the recognition they receive, their organizations typically have lower turnover and higher productivity and profitability than other organizations in the same industry! During economic downturns, these organizations lay off fewer employees and, when they do have to reduce their work force, employee morale is far more resilient.

The companies that make *Fortune* magazine's annual list of the 100 Best Companies to Work For provide great examples of companies that offer many forms of effective recognition. According to Robert Levering, who along with Milton Moskowitz oversees the *Fortune* magazine Best Companies project, "No company can have a great place to work without having good ways to show appreciation to employees." Not only do the companies on the list do a good job of offering the kind of recognition employees value, these companies receive tremendous payback for their efforts. Levering and Moskowitz' research shows:

- Industry by industry, the companies on the list have 50 percent less turnover than their counterparts.
- Publicly traded companies on the list average 15 to 25 percent greater return for investors than the S&P 500 over three-, five-, and ten-year periods.

With results like these, the companies on the *Fortune* Best Companies list, as well as others such as Remedy Support Services, demonstrate expertise in the area of employee morale and recognition. Still others are mentioned in this book because they have departments, managers, or supervisors who excel at recognizing their people, regardless of the level of recognition offered by their organization as a whole. Each offers an example that will help you understand what it takes to create meaningful recognition.

In the chapters that follow, you will learn how to create meaningful and memorable recognition that improves employee commitment to your organization. You will learn how to offer recognition that works and will begin to look at recognition differently. You will train yourself to see what the recipient sees, looking past superficial symbols and focusing on what really matters. In the process, you will reduce your workload, improve productivity, and create a workplace where people love to work!

PART 1

Employees Want to Love Their Work

chapter 1

Recognition That Works

"Please, not another T-shirt!"

"I resent the money that's spent to purchase doodads. It could be spent much more wisely."

"Certificates of appreciation? I hate the damn things."

These are the comments of real employees who say they aren't receiving enough recognition. If you asked the employees you manage about the recognition they receive, would they say something similar? If you depend on your organization to fulfill your employees' need for recognition, the answer is probably "yes."

According to a former employee of one technology company, "Our company offered the Terrific Employee Award. Everyone thought it was a cheesy name. People didn't know why they were being awarded. It became a joke. The CEO never got involved. No one but HR took it seriously. They solicited employees for nominations and got so few responses they eventually gave up and selected someone themselves. The awards were gift certificates. They were nice, but without meaning."

When Recognition Misses the Mark

When you think of recognition, what comes to mind? Do you think of raises, bonuses, stock awards, gift certificates, parties, prizes, and plaques? Many managers view these things as recognition. Employees have a different viewpoint. Like the employee in the last example, they are looking for meaning. They see tangible awards as a vehicle for *delivering* recognition, but they don't see the awards themselves as recognition. They're much more interested in the underlying message behind the reward.

Employees are strong believers in the old saying, "It's the thought that counts," and for awards to count as recognition, employees need to see acknowledgment of their specific accomplishments and sincere appreciation of their personal value to the organization. The following examples will illustrate why recognition often misses the mark.

Tangible Awards Aren't Recognition

Perks aren't recognition. The director of a small nonprofit agency hosts a dinner on a Friday night for employees and volunteers. Everyone has a great time and goes back to work the following Monday feeling refreshed and energized. The director planned this event as a form of recognition. Although it was fun and boosted morale, it wasn't recognition; it was a perk—a little something extra.

To add an element of recognition, the director can announce that the dinner is a way of thanking the group for something they have accomplished, for example, "We served ten thousand clients this year, and we couldn't have done it without your help." She can include an after-dinner presentation during which she tells detailed stories about the specific ways in which employees and volunteers helped to accomplish this feat. These things will provide recognition.

Bonuses aren't recognition. The owner of an insurance agency gives holiday bonuses. They come in handy when employees head out to do their last-minute shopping. Employees appreciate the bonus but don't see it as recognition. They expect it and feel entitled to it. Many have already budgeted for it, and if it is less than they anticipated, employees are resentful. If the bonus is more than was expected, they're pleasantly surprised but figure they must have earned it.

The owner of the agency thinks the bonuses are a form of recognition, but employees don't agree. To provide recognition, the owner needs to tie the bonuses to an achievement. But that isn't enough. He also needs to state that the bonuses are his way of showing appreciation: "Our customer service ratings are up 10 percent over last year. That increase has helped us to better position ourselves in the market. I know we couldn't have done it without all of your hard work, and I want to show my appreciation by giving each of you a seventy-five dollar bonus." Without the tie-in and the statement of appreciation, the bonus is just another way in which employees get paid.

Incentives aren't recognition. A manufacturer sets up a quota system for assemblers: When they reach a certain level, they will receive a one-hundred-dollar gift certificate. As assemblers reach their quota, they find their certificate tucked in their pay envelope. Their supervisor thinks the certificates are recognition, but they aren't. They are incentives. They tell employees, "If you do this, you will get that." Used properly, incentives can motivate people to do more, but there really isn't much recognition built in.

The line supervisor can easily add an element of recognition to the incentive. If he hand-delivers the certificate, personally congratulates the recipients, and offers appreciation for a job well-done, then the incentive will have recognition value.

Plaques and awards aren't always recognition. Each month in a staff meeting, the manager of a city public works department presents one employee with a plaque and a gift certificate. As she hands out the awards, she explains that the recipient is "doing a good job" and is a "great employee." She believes she is recognizing employees, but employees in her department have no idea what it takes to get the award. This public award is supposed to be recognition, but these employees see it as favoritism and feel even less recognized. If employees, including the recipients, don't understand why recognition is given, then recognition hasn't taken place.

If this manager establishes criteria for the award such as excellence in customer service or cost cutting, and then describes what the recipient did to earn the award, then the award will provide recognition.

There's a lot you can do that will make people feel recognized, but first you have to be clear about what recognition *isn't*. It isn't incentives, perks, or awards. While these things aren't recognition, they can be a highly valued part of the recognition experience. They can serve as excellent concrete reminders of the recognition you offer. An employee who does customer support offers the following example:

> "I was given a tough customer to assist. The underlying message was 'We don't entrust really important relationships to just anybody. We believe in you. You have proven yourself.' After I was successful, they let me pick from a catalog of gifts. The opportunity was the recognition, but the mixer I selected reminds me of it—every time I walk into the kitchen."

Don't make the mistake of thinking that the reminders are the recognition. If you do, you will fall into a common trap: assuming that all you need to make recognition work is a new award. Focus only on the tangible award and recognition will most likely fail. Focus on the *meaning* behind the award, and employees will receive recognition that works.

This isn't to say that looking for new award ideas doesn't have value. It's always a good idea to come up with new and creative ways to show recognition. There are excellent books that are filled with great recognition ideas. *1001 Ways to Reward Employees*[1] by Bob Nelson, and *301 Ways to Have Fun at Work*[2] by Dave Hemsath and Leslie Yerkes are two that I would recommend. There is nothing wrong with getting ideas. Just remember to probe a little deeper and ask yourself a few questions. What achievement does the award recognize? How are the recipients selected? When and how are awards presented? What does the manager do to make sure that the award provides recognition?

What Makes Recognition Work

Throughout this book you will read about recognition that works—the kind of recognition that inspires someone to say, "You made my day." Recognition that works is both memorable and meaningful. It stands out in employees' minds, sometimes because it's clever and unique, sometimes because of the consistency and regularity with which it is offered, and sometimes simply because it was heartfelt.

Recognition that works doesn't have to be difficult or complicated. It's a thank-you delivered in front of a group, one to one, or by e-mail. It's the written or verbal acknowledgement of an accomplishment. It's demonstrating a person's value to the organization by providing a new opportunity. Employees say small gestures mean the most.

Look up the words *recognize* or *recognition* in any dictionary and you will find definitions that use words like "see," "identify," and "acknowledge." These words are at the core of how employees define recognition. One man told me, "I'd be happy if I thought anyone here even knew I existed." Most employees don't feel anywhere near this level of dissatisfaction, but his comment does show the extreme of what it means to feel completely unrecognized.

Employees want to be seen—sometimes literally. When anyone higher up the organizational ladder greets an employee by name in the hallway, typically that employee will view the greeting as a form of recognition. Why? Because these are the people who employees most want to be seen by because they have the most influence over their careers.

Employees also want their accomplishments identified and acknowledged. When coworkers, internal customers, managers, and supervisors provide specific details about the value of an employee's contribution, they provide recognition that works at its most fundamental level.

Four Elements of Recognition That Works

So how do you offer recognition that works? You make sure it includes at least one of the four basic elements of meaningful recognition. If you don't include at least one of the elements, you aren't giving recognition. You're giving an incentive, prize, gift, or plaque, but not recognition that works. The four elements are praise, thanks, opportunity, and respect. Recognition that works is typically a combination of more than one of these four elements. Let's look at each element separately.

Praise

Employees want to hear you say, "Hey, you accomplished something important." They want you to acknowledge their progress. They want you to see what they do right.

Three tips for offering praise:

1) Be clear and concise about what you are praising.

2) Make the praise proportional to the accomplishment. Don't exaggerate or overdo it.
3) Keep it timely. Don't wait six months for the performance review. When you see it, praise it.

You can praise employees publicly or privately. Be aware that while every employee wants praise, not all employees want public praise. It's up to you to learn each employee's preference. For more on this, *see* chapter 11.

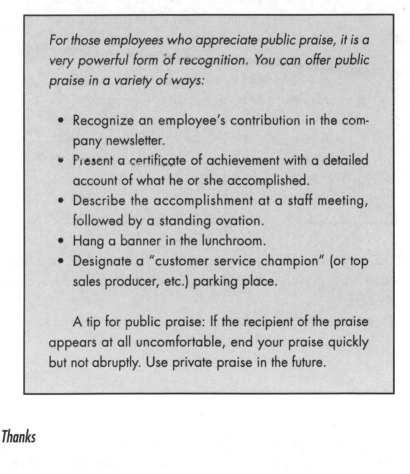

For those employees who appreciate public praise, it is a very powerful form of recognition. You can offer public praise in a variety of ways:

- Recognize an employee's contribution in the company newsletter.
- Present a certificate of achievement with a detailed account of what he or she accomplished.
- Describe the accomplishment at a staff meeting, followed by a standing ovation.
- Hang a banner in the lunchroom.
- Designate a "customer service champion" (or top sales producer, etc.) parking place.

A tip for public praise: If the recipient of the praise appears at all uncomfortable, end your praise quickly but not abruptly. Use private praise in the future.

Thanks

A sincere thank-you is a highly valued form of recognition that works. Some managers think there is no need to thank a person who is doing his or her job. It's true that you don't have to thank each employee, but if their efforts make your job easier, then thank him or her. Everyone responds to heartfelt appreciation. Employees will work many times harder for managers who express their gratitude. Offer a sincere thank-you, and you will make significant progress in improving morale and productivity.

Use a little variety when saying thanks.

Say "thank you" face to face with a smile, a handshake, and an explanation of how the employee helped you. Do this privately or publicly, depending of the employee's preference.

Give a hand-written note. Hand-written notes offer a personal touch. For those employees who save notes (and many do) this is a long-lasting form of recognition.

In some cases it's a novelty to send your thank-you by e-mail, fax, or express mail. When you want to have greater impact, use a method that will stand out from regular correspondence.

To make sure that your thank-you has the desired effect, describe why they are being thanked. Be specific, accurate, clear, and concise.

Remember: The simplest and frequently most desired form of recognition is a simple expression of gratitude.

Opportunity

At first glance, opportunity doesn't appear to be an element of recognition, but it's actually a very important element of recognition that works. Give your employees new opportunities to contribute in a meaningful way and learn new skills, provide them with more freedom in how the work gets done, and they will be committed to you and your department's success.

A few opportunities that provide recognition:

Ask employees for their opinion on critical issues. Include them in the decision-making process, and you recognize that they make a valuable contribution.

Give employees more control over projects. Recognize their contribution to the last project by giving them more responsibility on the next one.

Have employees select their own professional development courses and seminars. Give them the opportunity to determine what skills they need to develop.

Allow your employees to determine their own hours, so long as the work gets done. This recognizes their ability to work effectively with little supervision.

Give employees the opportunity to train or coach other employees.

Spend time with employees to learn about their workplace aspirations. Assess their ability and desire to work effectively with little supervision. Coach them on what they need to do to achieve their goals. Offer learning opportunities that will help them reach those goals. Increase their freedom in incremental stages as they demonstrate their ability to work well on their own. The results will be happy, productive employees who never want to leave!

Respect

Respect is an often overlooked element of recognition. In reality, it is probably the most crucial element. Without it, employees feel, at best, half recognized. Employees want to be valued, not just for what they can do, but for who they are. Consider employee needs as you make decisions, and you recognize employee value. Provide a safe, pleasant work environment, make allowance for personal crises, get to know something about each person who works with you, and you show respect.

Praise, thanks, opportunity, and respect are the four elements of recognition that works. Focus on these, and you will offer meaningful, memorable recognition that boosts morale and productivity.

TAKING ACTION

Here are a few things you can do to ensure that you offer recognition that works.

- Look at existing recognition programs for their true recognition value. Are they focused on an award or the four elements of recognition? Make sure employees feel like you are seeing and acknowledging them. Look for ways to simplify. You don't have to be clever—just sincere.
- Assess all tangible awards for recognition potential. Just because the incentives, perks, and celebrations aren't—in and of themselves—recognition doesn't mean you can't add an element of recognition to make them more meaningful.
- Continue reading for more ways to make their day!

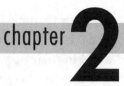

Recognition Is Inherent in the Work

Company recruiters visit college campuses every year. They want to lure the best and the brightest to their organizations. They paint a rosy picture of what awaits these college graduates. Recruiters tell these potential hires that they will be a valuable part of their team if only they will choose to work for them. Once hired, these new employees often find the situation a little different from what the recruiters described. Only a small percentage of organizations demonstrate, in any meaningful way, that they really believe the positive things their recruiters say to lure new hires.

Plante & Moran, a Michigan-based midsized accounting firm, is an exception. Its new hires know from the moment they arrive that they're valued. On their first day of work, new recruits receive business cards, manuals that will help them do their job well, and their own office with their name outside the door. They're assigned two people: one a supervising partner, and the other an experienced coworker called a "buddy." These two people help them adapt to work life and excel in their new careers. Plante & Moran provides concrete recognition of the value of new employees from the moment they are hired.

Employees see recognition in small gestures like receiving a nameplate on their first day and in bigger gestures like having a partner assigned to help them thrive and excel. The Plante & Moran new-hire process addresses the need for both respect and opportunity, two of the four elements of recognition. Employees there know they are valued. They know they are part of an organization where management wants to help them succeed.

Every day employees everywhere look for proof they are valued. Not only do they want their managers to tell them they are important, they want them to show it. They want to work for a manager who builds recognition into everyday occurrences. They want to work where recognition is inherent in the way they are treated and in the work they do.

It takes planning, preparation, and follow-through to make recognition part of the environment itself. The new-hire orientation at Plante & Moran is one example of how an organization does this. There are examples in this chapter of how an individual manager can create inherent recognition. First let's take a brief look at motivation theory and how it impacts your ability to recognize employees.

The Motivation Connection

Motivation can be intrinsic, extrinsic, or some combination of the two. Extrinsic motivation comes from outside of the individual. Extrinsic motivators are the incentives that you can offer: the promise of a bonus if certain criteria are met, the prize in a contest, and the lure of a raise if a project is completed on time. Used properly, these types of incentives can work well,[1] but there isn't much recognition built into them.

Used improperly, incentives damage motivation. One seminar participant told me, "I have a supervisor who complains about employees in our unit and then gives them a cash award in hopes that they will improve. What she should be doing is working to get rid of them." This supervisor has damaged employee trust and is no longer respected. Employees in her department are less likely to feel motivated to perform.

In contrast to extrinsic motivation, intrinsic motivation comes from within. Individuals motivate themselves based on their own personal needs and expectations. Intrinsic motivation varies from person to person with each individual being motivated by something slightly different from anyone else. A model of intrinsic motivation developed by David McClelland[2] says that what motivates us falls into three basic categories:

- **Achievement.** People motivated by achievement want to do something important or create something of value. They want to be valued for what they do.
- **Affiliation.** People motivated by affiliation want to belong. They want to be part of something bigger than themselves. They want to be valued for who they are and the company they keep.
- **Power/control.** People motivated by power and control want to have an impact on others or the environment. They want to be valued for how they change the world.

In varying degrees, these three motivators drive all of us. A biotech scientist might find motivation in her desire to make a discovery that would have an impact on the health and well-being of cancer victims. She would be more motivated by achievement and power/control and less by affiliation. A line worker might care more about producing quality work (achievement) and belonging to a team (affiliation) than by having an impact on people or the environment (power/control).

As a manager you can control some of the incentives and rewards used to motivate extrinsically, but can you do anything to affect intrinsic motivation? Absolutely! What effective recognition does best is acknowledge and support people's intrinsic motivators, and inherent recognition—recognition that comes from the work and workplace—often does this best. For instance, the biotech scientist from our previous example would see additional funding for her research as a valuable form of recognition because it validates the importance of her work. Her manager's efforts to get project funding, whether successful or not, recognize her potential to achieve and her ability to make a difference. The primary purpose of securing funding is to go forward with the research, not to recognize the employee. Yet the employee will feel recognized. That is inherent recognition—recognition that is built right into the work and workplace.

For the line worker who is motivated by affiliation and achievement, the supervisor can have a positive impact by supporting the team in its efforts to improve performance. The line supervisor might support his team when they suggest a change in workflow in order to reduce the defect rate simply because he wants to see a reduction in the defect rate. Yet the employee motivated by affiliation and achievement will feel recognized because of the inherent recognition that comes from the supervisor's support.

Orientation at Plante & Moran touches on all three intrinsic motivators. The new hire's "buddy" is a peer who provides the first link for affiliation with coworkers. The assigned partner guides the new hire in his or her quest for achievement and power/control.

Although Plante & Moran's treatment of new hires happens organization-wide, you can duplicate the inherent recognition in this experience by making new employees feel welcome and important. Introduce them to the rest of the team, assign a coworker to show them around, let them know that you are available for questions, and make sure they have everything they need to get started. You will offer strong intrinsic motivation for high performance.

Recognizing Purpose and Quality

Knowing what you're expected to achieve and what your department or organization as a whole hopes to achieve is very motivating. Purpose is a powerful motivator. The inherent recognition in purpose comes from seeing progress toward goals. Just ask the employees of most nonprofit agencies devoted to providing social services. If they know what their agency is trying to achieve and they believe they are making a contribution to those goals, they feel a strong sense of satisfaction. Many work willingly for much lower pay than they would in private industry because they believe they're making a difference.

You have probably heard more than a few jokes that make fun of the bureaucracy of some large organizations. But it's no longer funny when you find yourself having to deal with a bureaucratic agency or giant conglomerate. Have you ever experienced a situation where you had a problem and couldn't get anyone to help you? Did employees recite policies that made no sense? Did they shuffle you from department to department until you became frustrated by their lack of concern and caring? Coping with a bureaucracy can quickly wear you down.

Imagine how unmotivated the employees in these organizations must feel. They have to work all day, every day in an environment that frustrates and drains *you* in only a matter of moments. In this type of atmosphere, it is difficult to retain a sense of purpose. There is little motivation to do good work. Employees are disconnected from the recognition that is inherent in doing valued work.

Compare that to the Frederick Douglass Academy in Harlem.[3] When this public school was started in 1991, it replaced a bureaucratic public middle school. The academy was set up as a six-year school, serving as both a middle and high school. Its goal was to prepare students for college with an academically rigorous program. This new school accepted students with similar ethnic backgrounds and performance levels as students at other schools in the area.

What made Frederick Douglass Academy different from most other New York City schools were the guiding principles and vision of principal Lorraine Monroe. She kept teachers and students focused on what was important—learning—and refused to let them get bogged down by the system and what she referred to as "administrivia." She told teachers, "Don't be afraid to break rules, but do it only for the sake of the mission."

Teachers were very clear regarding their purpose. In fact they were so enthusiastic they volunteered to take on extra work just to see the school succeed. And succeed they did. When the first class graduated in 1997, 96 percent of the students were *accepted to college*. Compare that to an overall citywide high-school *graduation* rate of less than 70 percent.

These teachers knew what they were supposed to accomplish, knew they were capable of accomplishing it, and knew they had the support of their principal. That knowledge motivated them. The ultimate recognition was seeing their first class of students head off to college.

Employees want to take pride in their organization. They receive a form of recognition when they say, "I work for XYZ company," when XYZ company has a reputation for serving its community and producing quality products and services. In the survey employees completed for *Fortune* magazine's "100 Best Places to Work" list in 2001, 99 percent of Immunex employees said they were proud to tell others they work there. I asked Beth Fortmueller, Director of Human Resources at Immunex, why she thought that was true. She mentioned company values and mission. She said the purpose of their company is to create innovative treatments that help people. Over the past twenty years, the company has brought to market a number of new drugs that treat arthritis and cancer. Employees are proud of that record.

Every job, unless it's illegal or immoral, can have a mission or purpose that makes work meaningful and creates inherent recognition.

While your company may not be looking for a cure for cancer, the employees in your group can still develop pride in what they do. Consider the employees who work the counter at the Department of Motor Vehicles. Many DMV offices act as purposeless bureaucracies with unengaged workers. Within that environment, a dynamic supervisor can still motivate employees by helping them recognize how they contribute to the public good. Suddenly those same workers aren't just shuffling papers, they are doing their part to make the streets safe for the public by testing drivers' knowledge, verifying that drivers are insured, and requiring proof that vehicles don't spew pollutants.

What if you're the broker of a real estate office? Do your agents and employees simply deal in property sales, or do they help people fulfill their dreams of owning a home? If you help them identify a purpose that creates a sense of pride, you have helped to develop inherent recognition. Agents and employees with a higher purpose are far more likely to be enthusiastic and meticulous in their work. There is far more recognition in helping people fulfill their dreams than there is in selling houses.

Regardless of what your group does, it has a worthwhile purpose. Help your people find that purpose. Help them provide services or products of exceptional quality. Continually work to improve the group's reputation within the organization and your community. Remember that one of the elements of recognition is opportunity. Give employees the opportunity to contribute in a meaningful way. Acknowledge their progress. This will create inherent recognition. When people are part of a team that knows that their work is making a difference, they receive recognition that works.

Recognizing Trustworthiness

People want to be trusted to do the right thing. Managers who demonstrate trust by providing unlimited access to information, giving employees the freedom to work flexible hours, telework, make decisions without someone's approval, or do the job as they see fit so long as they meet objectives are recognizing that employees have the best interests of the organization at heart and can be trusted to do what is right. Trusting employees provides two elements of recognition: respect and opportunity.

Athleta is a small catalog company that also manufactures women's athletic wear. When Scott Kerslake, president and CEO, started the company four years ago, he created an organization where employees control their own work and time. If a customer service member needs to pick up kids from school during their shift, they simply arrange for coverage. If someone doesn't have childcare, they can bring their kids to work. Employees are encouraged to take long lunch breaks so they can participate in athletic activities. Many work split shifts. They have the opportunity to create their own work schedules because they are respected as trustworthy individuals.

Kerslake and his executive team believe that to provide this kind of freedom you have to have strong performance standards. They focus on individual and team responsibility. When they make hiring decisions, they look for people who they believe will meet their performance standards. Then they hold people personally accountable for meeting those standards. Beyond that, employees are primarily responsible for deciding when and how the work gets done. Does this strategy work? It does. Athleta averages about 5 percent annual turnover, compared to 30 percent in their industry.

Recognizing Individual Value

Opportunities for Growth

Employees want to be recognized for their achievements, but they also want to know they are valued as people—that they are respected for who they are, not just what they do. One way you show employees they are valued is by paying close attention to what they need and then helping them meet those needs. The freedom and flexibility at Althleta shows employees they are valued. Providing opportunities for growth does this as well.

The people at Plante & Moran know they are valued, in part, because the organization does such an exceptional job of helping people learn, develop, and grow. Managers focus on retaining people by meeting their need for new opportunities and challenges. They recognize people's value by ensuring that they are doing a job that provides satisfaction. In order to do this, employees are encouraged to use Plante & Moran's in-house vocational counselors. If someone is bored with auditing, the vocational counselors will help him find a new challenge appropriate to his skills, aptitude, and interests. Usually employees are able to stay within the company, perhaps moving to a position where they offer investment advice, expert testimony, or handle mergers and acquisitions. Occasionally, employees discover a passion that just can't be filled within an accounting firm. Plante & Moran's vocational counselors still assist these employees in the process and have, on occasion, counseled employees who go on to become doctors, priests, and, even in one case, a disc jockey. They lose a few people, but at the same time they develop a reputation of truly having their employees' best interests at heart.

Bill Bufe, Plante & Moran's Human Resources Director, joined the company directly out of college with a major in accounting. He started as an auditor, but it wasn't long before he realized he had a knack for recruiting and training. As he expressed interest in this area, he found his responsibilities gradually shifting. Over time he moved from audit partner to human resources. His responsibilities changed as his interests changed. Thirty-two years later, he is still with the company because he knows he is valued. Employees know the management at Plante & Moran wants them to do what they love and what they do best. It is one of the ways the management demonstrates that employees are important. It is one of the ways they provide inherent recognition.

Because the average employee changes jobs every few years, managers typically feel less of an obligation to provide growth opportunities to their employees than did their predecessors a few decades ago. Ironically, one of the reasons people leave is to pursue new growth opportunities. According to a study by WorldatWork and Nextera's Sibson Consulting Group, only 68 percent of employees are satisfied with the career opportunities they are provided.[4] If managers focused more attention on creating new opportunities for their employees, they could reduce turnover and increase inherent recognition.

To improve both retention and enthusiasm, help employees take on new and different responsibilities. Recognize employees' value to the organization by giving them opportunities to grow and learn. Invest your time and budget in helping employees develop skills that will move them forward in their careers—even if your department won't benefit directly from those skills. The more opportunities for growth you provide, the greater your reputation for developing people. You will attract people who particularly value this form of recognition—people who will work hard to make your department successful.

Pay and Benefits

Pay and benefits demonstrate individual value. Pay people less than they're worth and less than others in similar positions are paid, and they will interpret that to mean, "You don't matter to us." Underpaying employees will lead them to feel exploited and undervalued. Common benefits such as health insurance and vacation have an impact similar to fair pay. Provide less than is customary, and employees feel undervalued. According to Frederick Herzberg,[5] pay and benefits don't motivate, but their lack can cause dissatisfaction. In the same regard, people really don't think of pay and benefits as recognition, but they can see their absence as a lack of recognition.

Other benefits, particularly those that are less commonplace, can have more recognition value because they tell people they are special. JM Family Enterprises, a family-owned business in Deerfield, Florida, offers some unique benefits. This company of thirty-five hundred associates runs a Toyota distributorship and two related businesses. They have two corporate physicians, free medical exams, and free prescription drugs. They have an on-site barbershop and hair salon that offers free hair care and manicures. There is a fitness center, and a childcare center is being built. Not all employees use every benefit, but they see the value of them anyway. They see that management is committed to their well-being.

As a manager, you probably don't have a great deal of say in how much your group, as a whole, is paid. If your group is paid well or has outstanding benefits, talk to employees about how they are valued by both you and the organization. If they are underpaid or have limited benefits, you need to counteract the negative impact by explaining the situation as best you can. Maybe your company is going through hard times, and the situation is temporary. Maybe your company simply doesn't think that it has to meet industry standards. Whatever the reason, clarify that you think they are worth more than they are getting.

Work Environment

Do employees have the resources they need to do their work? Is their work area clean and safe? The work environment that you help create is another way that you tell employees that they are valued. Like pay and benefits, it's not so much that they see these things as recognition, rather they see a poor work environment as a lack of recognition of their value to you and the organization. Employees don't say, "Golly, I have all this information at my disposal, they must think I'm important." They don't spend much time thinking about the work environment—unless it's substandard. Then employees begin to question their importance to the organization. Public school teachers offer a classic example. Many teachers dig into their own paychecks to buy basic classroom supplies like paper and markers. When they have to do this, they're likely to think, "The district doesn't consider my work important." Is it any wonder many teachers feel undervalued?

Many elements of the work environment are out of a manager's control. School principals may have no budget for supplies, but that doesn't mean they can't work with parents, teachers, and community supporters to find a solution. Fire and police chiefs can't guarantee a work environment that is always safe. They can, however, work with their people to create as safe an environment as possible. Anything a manager does to improve the employee work environment—successful or not—will recognize employee value.

There is one element of the work environment within a manager's control. Every manager can influence team spirit. Managers are the primary influence as to whether the work environment is oppressive or supportive. To create a more positive environment you can introduce humor into the workday, have small celebrations, and encourage people to work together. People will enjoy being part of your group and will feel valued. They will recognize that you have their best interests in mind.

Recognition Is Everywhere

Anything that tells people they are valued and important has inherent recognition. It isn't all about perks and special benefits. It's about basic respect. A sixth-grade teacher told me that when he experienced a hearing loss, his principal refused to do anything to help him remain effective. Her indifference and lack of support showed him he wasn't valued. Ultimately, he resigned.

Recognition, or lack of it, really is inherent in everything we do. Keeping employees informed and updated recognizes their value. Providing the best possible work environment does the same thing. Consider the Plante & Moran philosophy: They believe they should re-recruit their employees every day. Bill Bufe describes re-recruiting this way, "Think of your best staff member. Think as if he is coming in to see you today. What would you do or say if he said he was leaving? Do those things anyway."

TAKING ACTION

- Provide appropriate opportunities. While you are delegating responsibilities, consider who has the appropriate skills *and* who would value a new opportunity.
- Clarify your organization's purpose and make sure employees understand their role in achieving that purpose.
- Provide the tools, resources, and information employees need to do their jobs effectively.
- Treat employees as if they have just said they are leaving. What will you do differently in order to keep them?

chapter 3

Recognition Is About Relationships

What makes recognition work? That's what I wanted to know when I began asking employees from around the country to tell me about memorable workplace recognition they had received. I wanted to hear directly from the people being recognized and get their reaction to the recognition efforts of their employers. I wanted to hear about the recognition experiences that had "made their day."

I solicited the opinions of employees all over the country and more than one hundred responded, describing recognition that had made their day. They also shared their recognition horror stories. You will find samples of both sprinkled throughout the book. These stories of both positive and negative recognition experiences provide insight into what matters to employees.

If your manager put a sticker on a report you had written, would that make an impression on you? Would that impression be positive or negative? Two women from two different companies each described having a sticker applied to a report that they had prepared. The stickers made a big impression. Each woman said that she would never forget how it felt to receive one. That's where the similarity ends. One described the sticker as an example of the types of silly things her manager does to motivate people. She and her coworkers thought the stickers were childish and embarrassing, an example of recognition with a negative impact. Their negative response might seem like the only reasonable reaction to receiving a sticker, except that the other woman told the story as an example of recognition with a positive impact. She said the stickers were highly valued in her company. They were both meaningful and memorable. Getting a sticker showed that your work was of exceptional quality. It was a little like getting a Pulitzer Prize.

Makes you want to shop at the second sticker store, doesn't it? If only it were that simple. Clearly, the form that recognition takes isn't what creates the impact. It isn't the quality of the sticker, nor is it simply a matter of difference in individual preference. If these women are representing their organizations in a fairly accurate manner, they share their opinions with the majority of their coworkers. So what is the difference? What makes one sticker valuable and the other absurd?

Further exploration of the sticker stories revealed a difference in the relationships that these two women had with the managers presenting the stickers. The second manager was highly regarded and had an excellent relationship with his employees. Any form of recognition he used, from candy bars to public praise, would probably have positive results. The other manager had never earned employee respect. Any form of recognition he used, including bonuses and promotions, would probably have failed. Employees would have still felt unrecognized.

Everything Else Is Secondary

With recognition, nothing is more important than the relationship between the giver and the receiver. You can structure an innovative and generous program. You can offer frequent, timely, and proportional recognition. You can plan a program that is technically flawless, but none of that matters if the people you are recognizing don't value your feedback. Next to relationships, everything else is secondary.

Managers who are most successful spend less time thinking about recognition itself and more time thinking about how they can help the people they work with. When they say that people are the most important asset, they mean it. They help others learn and grow. They share information and trust people to use it appropriately. They value both the individual and their contribution. People can tell when someone really cares about them. That can't be faked. When it comes to recognition that works, nothing can replace sincere respect and the positive relationships that it creates.

Consider your own work relationships. Do people trust you to have their best interests at heart? Whether you are aware of it or not, our colleagues and coworkers keep a kind of mental balance sheet on each of us. Steven Covey calls it an "emotional bank account."[1] I prefer "trust account." When you make a promise and follow through, you make a small deposit into your trust account. When you are honest and open, you make another deposit. Give an evasive answer or make inappropriate disclosures about other employees, and you write a large check. Listen poorly, offer insincere recognition, or represent yourself as an expert when you're not, and before you know it, that trust account is overdrawn, and the people you work with have stamped an imaginary NSF (Not Sufficient Funds) on your forehead. Your account is the reputation you build one person at a time. That reputation decides the quality of your relationships and the impact of your recognition.

If you have any doubts about the relationships you've built, forget about actively recognizing people for a while. Instead, work on the inherent recognition that comes with trust, respect, and caring. If you do this, you will strengthen the foundation that your relationships are built upon. Keep the best interests of employees and coworkers at heart, and the recognition that you offer will have a positive impact.

Employees Have Their Say

A director-level member of a network marketing organization told me that he had competed for his company's President's Circle Award.[2] After a year of hard work he won. He was the top sales producer for his region. At the annual conference, the president of the company presented him with a plaque. The director was very proud of his accomplishment and the organization-wide recognition that it offered. The experience would have been very positive and motivating, except that when he returned to his seat and looked at the plaque, he discovered that his name had been misspelled. Now he sensed that the award might not be as important to the president as it was to him, but he didn't want to jump to any conclusions. He told the president about the error and gave him the opportunity to make things right. The president could have repaired the situation by simply apologizing and getting the plaque corrected. Instead he responded, "Oh well . . ."

The president assumed that getting the top sales producer award was what mattered. What he didn't understand was that the director was more interested in how the award would affect their relationship. He assumed that, as the top sales producer, he was now a member of the organization's inner circle. He assumed that he and the president would have a new relationship and that the award was the formal announcement of that relationship to the rest of the organization.

When his name was misspelled it cast doubt on his assumptions, but he offered the president the opportunity to repair the situation and reconfirm that he valued their relationship. Instead, the president's lack of interest in rectifying the mistake made it clear to the director that their relationship was insignificant. Recognition from the president no longer has meaning for this director. While he may continue to be top sales producer for a while, his sense of loyalty to the organization is damaged. When a new job opportunity comes along, he will be much more likely to take it.

Relationships are the cornerstone of recognition. In interview after interview, this same theme kept replaying itself. Without trust, respect, and communication, recognition doesn't matter. With these things, nearly anything can become valued recognition. One woman told me that the president of her company had asked her to take his place on a panel discussion at an international conference. She said that this opportunity was one that she would never forget. That's understandable when you consider the underlying message that the request held for her. The president was highly respected in his field and with his employees. Without his saying so with words, the employee interpreted his request to mean that he considered her an expert in their field and that he trusted her to represent him. No wonder this opportunity made her day. If she had a poor relationship with the president, would she have interpreted the request the same way? Probably not. She would have wondered why he didn't want to go and why she was stuck taking his place.

Another person, who expressed a tremendous amount of loyalty for her supervisor, described herself as a sports fan. She told how, in her annual company-required performance evaluation, her supervisor broke the tension and showed respect for her and her interests in a playful way. Her supervisor's written evaluation used sports terminology to describe her performance. Phrases like "You really scored big" and "Shows an improved ability to tackle problems" communicated to her that her supervisor cared about both her and her performance.

Some respondents told of managers who let them work flexible hours or gave them control over how the work was completed. Others shared how supervisors helped them overcome obstacles, let them find their own way through obstacles, or selected roles for them that offered new and interesting challenges. Not everyone mentioned their managers or supervisors when they told of recognition that made their day. They also told stories of coworkers who shared credit for success on a project or offered appreciation for their assistance. There were dozens of very different responses to my questions about what makes recognition memorable and meaningful. The common thread throughout was that the person offering the recognition knew the recipient well enough to know what was wanted or needed and then provided it.

Fill the Other Guy's Basket to the Brim

Some organizations seem to have an almost intuitive understanding about workplace relationships. When you enter one of these organizations you get a sense that everyone likes, trusts, and respects the people they work with. These organizations have a reputation as a great place to work. They have their choice of the best employees in their industries. They have no trouble recruiting or retaining, even while others struggle. They get consistently high job satisfaction ratings from their employees, and employees go out of their way to find ways to improve their products, services, and work environment. Recognition in these organizations reinforces the positive relationships that have already been built.

At Dallas-based retailer The Container Store, 97 percent of employees agree with the survey statement, "People care about each other here." The company has made respect for employees a cornerstone of their philosophy. They show that respect in a number of ways. Even with twenty-five stores, the executive team still knows most full-time employees by name. Part-timers are known as prime-timers, and employee salaries are well above industry average. Everything they do, individually and as an organization, is meant to acknowledge the vital role that all employees play in the success of the company.

Number one on *Fortune* Magazine's 100 Best Companies to Work For list two years in a row, dropping only to number two in their third year, The Container Store rates consistently high in employee satisfaction. They have a turnover rate of 20 to 25 percent in an industry where annual turnover of over 100 percent is common, and a full 41 percent of new hires come from employee referrals. Reduced costs associated with recruiting and hiring mean the company is able to pay higher salaries than the industry average and still experience 20 percent sales growth each year.

At The Container Store they believe that everyone should "fill the other guy's basket to the brim." It's a memorable image for a retailer, one that suggests that everyone is responsible for making sure that both customers and coworkers get what they need. Employees live this philosophy. Elizabeth Barrett, VP of Operations, shared an example that illustrates this philosophy. A customer forgot her merchandise in the parking lot of one of their stores and later returned to retrieve it. When she found that it wasn't in the parking lot, she went into the store to see if it had been turned in. The customer was very upset to discover that it hadn't been. The employee whom she spoke with assessed the situation and literally "filled her basket to the brim," replacing the missing merchandise.

Make sure people get what they need. This philosophy doesn't mean that The Container Store employees give away the store, but it does mean that they take care of the customers and each other. Employees fill their coworkers' baskets to the brim in a variety of ways. They might grab a ladder from the stockroom for someone who is struggling with a ladder that is too small or fill in for someone who has to unexpectedly take a day off. You'll often overhear employees in all areas of the company saying, "Thanks for filling my basket!" It is all about helping one another any way that they can.

The executive team at The Container Store leads the way in living this philosophy. They are continually looking for new ways to fill employees' baskets to the brim. The following are just a few of the ways they have done this:

- They made the decision to "blow up HR," giving many of its responsibilities back to each store in order to strengthen the relationship between employees and their managers. They wanted employees to bring issues directly to their managers rather than to an intermediary.
- Garrett Boone, chairman and cofounder, meets personally with nearly all 599 full-time employees at least once each year to learn what they need in order to do their jobs better.
- The benefits director does a survey each winter to learn whether existing benefits are effective and to discover what new benefits would be most valued. Management acts quickly on the results of each survey.

When employees said that it was difficult to get through December and January, their busiest months, management listened. Employees said that they found the long hours and crowds of customers during that hectic time to be very physically and emotionally demanding. They wanted some kind of a break. Management provided that break when they decided that they would close their doors on New Year's Day, giving up sales for the sake of their employees.

The Container Store does a good job of demonstrating that, while relationships are between individuals, organizational structure and culture can also work to build relationships. They have developed a company culture that puts relationships first. The leadership sets a strong example, and managers and employees follow that example because they firmly believe in the philosophy. According to Jane Ellen Graham, Travel Manager, "I have never worked anywhere else where I felt appreciated every day! It is so nice to have people take the time to say thanks even though I'm just doing my job. It makes you want to always make the extra effort, because your fellow employees will do the same for you." Everyone in this company "Fills the Other Guy's Basket" with respect and recognition.

Strong Relationships Create Loyalty

The low turnover and solid growth rate at The Container Store demonstrate that strong relationships create a tremendous amount of employee loyalty. The correlation between turnover, relationship, and loyalty isn't unique to The Container Store. Most companies that put a high value on relationships enjoy a high level of employee loyalty. Xilinx, a semiconductor company based in San Jose, California, provides another example.

To build strong relationships, one of the most important things recognition should do is communicate that a person is valued. Xilinx does this in ways that employees find particularly meaningful. While many companies say they value employees and structure elaborate recognition programs to demonstrate that value, when hard times hit, the first thing they do is lay off 25 percent of their work force. This sends a conflicting message that damages relationships and causes morale to drop among those employees who remain. Managers at Xilinx, on the other hand, decided the best way they could demonstrate employee value was to avoid layoffs if at all possible.

According to Chris Taylor, Senior Director of Human Resources for Xilinx, when the semiconductor industry went into an economic slump in 2001, their leaders sat down and reassessed their company values. They decided that if they really respected people and really believed their people were their best resource, they should recognize that fact by finding alternate ways to scale back labor costs, reserving layoffs as their last resort.

Two thousand one was a tough year for most technology companies. Xilinx was no exception. By December, revenue was off 50 percent. What made Xilinx exceptional under these circumstances was that the company hadn't laid off a single employee. They could have chosen a more cost-effective short-term solution, but management believed that the long-term gain from having retained their highly valuable work force was worth the risk. Xilinx found other ways to reduce labor costs. Management started with a tiered pay cut, with the biggest earners taking the largest cut. Then there was an across-the-board pay cut, and finally a variety of voluntary programs to cut labor costs. They communicated their plans to employees each step of the way, never promising that layoffs wouldn't eventually become necessary, but demonstrating that layoffs would be the last resort.

This commitment to Xilinx employees was a powerful form of recognition. Management demonstrated just how valued their employees were. Employees responded with a tremendous amount of understanding and loyalty. Some offered to take even greater pay cuts than requested. The organization demonstrated employee value in a way that no recognition program could match. Through their commitment to retaining their people, even during difficult times, the leadership strengthened their relationship with every employee.

A strong relationship between employees and the leadership is nothing new at Xilinx. When CEO Wim Roelandts left Hewlett-Packard to join Xilinx in 1996, Xilinx was heading into a difficult time. Under his leadership, the company was able to gain momentum, surpassing their closest competitor in revenue. During the fiscal year that ended March 2000, they reached a milestone. They hit the billion-dollar mark. To show his gratitude, Roelandts gave every employee a bottle of champagne labeled Xilinx Billion Dollars. It came in a champagne bucket engraved with the individual's name. It was a nice gift, and because recognition goes both ways, employees wanted to thank him for his leadership. They decided to take out a full-page ad that read, "Wim Roelandts: Thanks a Billion for Your Leadership!" Behind the bold-print headline, in faint print was the name of every employee in the organization. When employees showed their CEO the ad at a company meeting, there was a five-minute standing ovation. Roelandts was choked up. Even CEOs love recognition.

Strong bonds between employees at all levels create powerful company loyalty. Building strong bonds means building trust. Building trust means developing respect and cooperation. In organizations where strong relationships are valued, everyone works hard to maintain these things and is careful not to do anything to damage those relationships.

The Danger of Intra-Company Competition

Competition is one of the most common ways in which managers and organizations can damage relationships. Lots of organizations, divisions, and departments stage competitions. After all, contests between departments, teams, and individuals seem like a fun way to achieve a goal. Sports pit teams against each other, and people enjoy the competition, so why not enjoy that same spirit of competition at work? The difference is that in sports, opposing teams aren't expected to work together or cooperate and collaborate after the competition. High-stakes competition often creates animosity between competitors, which damages relationships and makes working together difficult. Consider the following situation:

> A small manufacturer of bath products holds a production contest. The morning and evening shifts compete to see who produces the most during the quarter. The prize is a three-hundred-dollar bonus for everyone on the production shift: line workers, members of the maintenance crew, and the shift supervisor. At the end of the first week, production is up. Line workers are working faster and smarter. Changes to the line that will improve performance are suggested. So far so good.

As the second week comes to a close, management learns that production levels have stalled. They give both shifts a pep talk, trying to motivate them to find innovative ways to increase production. Workers push for ways to outpace their competitors. They skip routine maintenance, withhold information, hoard supplies, and do their best to make production impossible for the other crew. Cooperation that once existed is now gone. Nobody wins.

It is possible to compete successfully without damaging relationships if you do a couple of things differently.

- Don't compete for high-stake rewards. Keep competitions fun by keeping the prizes fun. People aren't as likely to toss out the relationships that they've built for a pizza party as they are for a three-hundred-dollar bonus.
- Compete to beat past measures, such as improving on a safety record, beating a sales goal, or improving a customer satisfaction rating. Multiple winners should be possible.

You can have successful intra-company competitions without damaging relationships, but only if you work hard to ensure that those relationships remain intact. Competition has to be secondary to maintaining the bonds between employees. Focus on what matters most.

How Do You Measure Up?

Do you focus on what matters most? Ask yourself whether the people you work with value the recognition that you already give. Have you developed mutual trust, respect, and loyalty with them? How about the rest of your organization? Does it measure up? Do employees throughout the organization value the relationships that they have with their managers, their coworkers, and with the organization in general? Recognition that works has more to do with trust, respect, loyalty, and creating strong relationships than it does with contests, programs, or awards. Without healthy working relationships, recognition is meaningless. It is up to you to create an atmosphere of trust, respect, and loyalty where recognition can thrive.

TAKING ACTION

- Assess your relationships with the people you work with. If your relationships are damaged, recognition will be meaningless. Build strong relationships first, then you can explore other ways to recognize people.
- Assess how your organization demonstrates the value of relationships. Look for ways that you can build trust and respect into the organizational culture. If you're unable to influence organizational behavior any other way, work to improve the relationships within your department or unit. Model behavior that creates strong working relationships.
- Regardless of your role in your organization, you can show recognition by treating individuals as the valuable people they are. Find ways to help others. As The Container Store employees would say, "Fill their baskets to the brim."

PART 2

Recognition—Whose Job Is It Anyway?

chapter **4**

Managers and Supervisors Have the Greatest Impact

Ask one hundred employees what their favorite form of recognition is, and you will get at least fifty different answers. Ask the same one hundred employees *who* they most want to receive recognition from, and the majority will say they want it from their manager or supervisor. Organizational recognition is important; for some employees it's necessary for promotion. Recognition from the leadership or senior management can make a big impression and reinforce important values. Recognition from peers is appreciated because it enhances the sense of teamwork and camaraderie and often comes from the people who understand the work best. Even though all these sources of recognition are important, they don't carry the same weight as recognition that comes from the manager.

Athleta, the women's sportswear company profiled in chapter 2, provides inherent recognition by trusting employees and providing a great deal of autonomy. They also encourage community involvement, which provides its own recognition. Employees volunteer in support of women's athletics and participate in events themselves. Through this participation, they experience recognition from their community.

Employees at Athleta are a close-knit group. The company culture is so strong a draw that Athleta only experiences about 5 percent turnover each year. Yet, according to Rick Scott, Director of Team Support, many forms of recognition are missing at Athleta. Few managers coach or train employees or work to provide them with appropriate new opportunities. Managers do little to specifically address the recognition needs of employees.

Athleta is a fairly new company. Scott says they are at a critical stage in their development. They have grown to a point where they need to address these issues soon or people will begin to leave. For example, a recent survey of Athleta employees showed less than 50 percent satisfaction with recognition overall. Although the organizational culture and the support of both leadership and peers provide some recognition, the missing component is recognition that comes from an employee's manager or supervisor. The survey confirmed what senior management suspected. They need to train managers and supervisors to better meet the recognition needs of their employees. Today they are working to meet that need.

Opportunity and Responsibility

As a manager or supervisor you are most able to provide the recognition that employees crave. Recognition that you offer reassures employees that they are performing up to expectations. Employees want recognition from the person with the most control over their career. According to an employee of a large healthcare provider,

"Recognition from my manager is most important because he's the one doing my annual review, not the organization or my coworkers. He's the one likely to recommend me for a promotion." Even those who say they prefer peer recognition see it, at least in part, as a way to secure recognition from management. As one employee stated, "The praise of coworkers can sometimes lead to praise from management. If management is listening, then they will hear your coworkers sing your praises and perhaps look at you in a different light." As a manager or supervisor, you have the greatest opportunity and responsibility for providing employee recognition.

Opportunity

No one is in a better position to offer consistent, meaningful recognition than the employee's manager or supervisor. They have knowledge and opportunities that others just don't have.

Managers should have the most comprehensive information on what employees are accomplishing.

Managers usually have access to any recognition budget that is available.

Managers always have an opportunity to learn about how each employee wants to be recognized.

Managers should have knowledge about whether or not employees are receiving frequent, timely, and appropriate recognition from all sources combined.

Managers typically have the greatest opportunity to coach employees on how to provide self-recognition (*see* chapter 8).

Managers generally have the ear of upper management. Managers and supervisors can recognize employees in a way that improves employees' visibility and increases their chances of promotion.

Managers should have a high-profile role in their departments or divisions and be in the best position to model good recognition behavior and encourage peer recognition.

Responsibility

As a manager, you represent the organization. Particularly in large organizations, employees tend to blur the distinction between manager and organization. A study by Maritz Research[1] found a strong correlation between employee support for the company's products and services and their perception of their managers. One question in the study asked employees if their managers "walk the talk." The other asked if employees support their company's products and services. Ninety percent of the employees who responded that their managers do "walk the talk" also expressed support for their company's products and services. Of those who answered that their managers do not "walk the talk," only 25 percent expressed support for the company's products and services. In the eyes of employees, the manager is the organization. If managers don't recognize employees, most employees will say that the organization, in general, doesn't recognize them.

Missed Opportunity

Managers and supervisors have the opportunity and means to create recognition that offers the greatest impact. Yet, according to the Kepner-Tregoe study mentioned in the preface, only 40 percent of workers and less than 50 percent of managers and supervisors said employees receive recognition for high performance. Is it any wonder employees feel unrecognized? Most managers know that their employees want more recognition, yet they resist for a variety of reasons.

They resist because they believe that being paid is the only recognition employees need. In their view, employees are motivated by money. They think recognition isn't necessary and can lead employees to expect more money. The truth is employees want recognition for its own sake.

They resist because they are too busy doing their job to spend time on recognition. It is common knowledge that managers and supervisors have too much to do. Many believe that the day-to-day challenges are difficult enough without adding recognition to their list of things to do. As mentioned in the introduction, this point of view is short-sighted. Employees who receive regular, quality recognition are more productive and self-directed. Employees who feel recognized make the manager's job easier, not harder.

They resist because they are afraid they will be accused of playing favorites. Favoritism is a very real concern that can be addressed by establishing sound criteria and then recognizing employees for progress in meeting those criteria. Consistency in recognizing valued behaviors is critical for creating a sense of fairness. *See* chapters 9 and 10 for more information on specific and measurable criteria.

They resist because they have experienced a program that failed miserably. Many managers and supervisors have observed recognition programs that were so poorly received they are reluctant to try again. An important point to remember is that very little real recognition comes from programs; it comes from people. A manager or supervisor's personal efforts to recognize employees will have a greater impact than any program.

They resist because their own attempts at recognition have failed. Managers and supervisors who don't understand what it takes to provide meaningful recognition are likely to get a response similar to this firsthand account from a workshop participant:

> "Twice our director gave out certificates of appreciation. I put both of mine in the recycling at home. He gave everyone the same certificate. I felt they didn't mean anything because he gave them to all 140 employees in the unit including: the person who doesn't perform most of his duties, the one who comes in late and leaves early nearly every day, and another who spends most of her time on the phone on personal business."

The only thing this manager recognized was that these were the people on his unit's payroll. He doesn't understand that recognition must be tied to performance and the value that each employee provides to the unit. In his attempt to be fair, he was unfair to those who work hard and act responsibly. After a few lackluster attempts, this manager will probably decide recognition doesn't work and quit trying. He has missed the opportunity to offer meaningful recognition because he doesn't understand what makes recognition work.

Laying the Foundation— The Manager/Employee Relationship

In chapter 3, "Recognition Is About Relationships," you learned that if the relationship between the employees and the people around them was damaged, recognition would have little impact or even the wrong impact. What wasn't mentioned was that the most important relationship is the one between managers and the people who report directly to them.

A university employee explains the power of making a personal connection. "The new dean sent me a birthday card with a handwritten note. I don't think I've had a boss do that in my professional life. Maybe a boss has added their name to a card from the staff, maybe they've said 'Happy Birthday' when they've seen balloons or cards at my desk, or maybe they chipped in for a gift. But to have a boss with far too many direct reports make a point of sending a card with a note was surprisingly touching. Such a small thing had such a big impact."

In chapter 2, "Recognition Is Inherent in the Work," you learned that employees can be recognized in many different ways: new challenges, training opportunities, and flexibility in scheduling, just to name a few. Many of the options and opportunities that create inherent recognition are under the control of the manager or supervisor. They can provide training and coaching opportunities based on employee strengths and interests. Often they can adjust employee schedules to allow workers to reduce the need for child-care or pursue a new hobby. They can stay on the lookout for new projects and challenges that will help their employees meet their career goals.

Employees also look to management for feedback on their performance. Well-phrased feedback, whether it is praise or suggestions for improvement, can be valuable recognition. For employees, feedback from a caring manager translates to coaching and development opportunities that will help them improve.

My husband, Gary, shared a story about a manager who he had very early in his career. Gary had gone to this manager to complain that he had too much work. He told the manager that he didn't have time to get it all done. Knowing that too much work wasn't the problem, his manager could have simply ignored the complaint. Instead, he recognized Gary's value to the organization by demonstrating his commitment to helping Gary improve. He helped Gary improve his own awareness by quietly pointing out the numerous times that week that he had seen Gary standing around chatting with coworkers. He suggested that if Gary instead used that time to tackle his outstanding projects, he would be able to finish his work. For the next few weeks, Gary caught himself each time he stopped to chat. He used that time as his manager suggested and found that he really was able to finish his work. His effectiveness grew because of his manager's feedback.

Negative feedback can be recognition. If feedback is offered with good intentions and framed as a development tool, most employees appreciate learning the hard lessons. They know that they have to improve and grow in order to progress. If employees seem to resent all corrective feedback, most likely it is because they aren't receiving enough of the positive kind. Many managers only speak to employees when there is a problem. To quote one employee, "Positive comments are usually few and far between." If managers only offer suggestions for improvement and don't recognize what their employees do well, then employees will tune them out.

Exceptional Managers

In preparing to write this book, I asked employees to tell me about managers who did an exceptional job of recognizing their people. Employees nominated managers from a variety of organizations. The three managers I selected came from companies with three diverse approaches to formal recognition: one company has very little formal recognition, another has formal recognition that hasn't been very effective, and the third has programs that are very well received. It is interesting to see how little the existing recognition environment affects how these three managers approach recognition.

Company #1

Jim Wheeler is an employee at Williams, an energy company in Tulsa, Oklahoma. He suggested that I interview his former manager, Michelle Boyes. When he worked for Boyes, she was Manager of Employee Learning and Development and led a team of eighteen people. According to Wheeler, "She exercised her remarkable talents in selecting and developing talent and facilitating high-performance teamwork in order to take our rag-tag bunch and turn us into a respected group of professionals." Not only did Wheeler believe that Boyes was a skilled manager, he was impressed at her ability to encourage recognition among the members of their team. In nominating her for inclusion in this chapter, Wheeler wrote:

> "Last year, after some very intensive work over a period of months, our entire team got together at a lakeside cabin. The opportunity to be in a casual setting away from the office with some good food was a reward in and of itself.

We ate breakfast and discussed the very large project we had just closed out. She gave a token of appreciation to each member of the team and had special prizes for three team members who had been selected by their peers for contributing the most effort.

The next part of the day was intended to only last an hour or so. Each person on the team would take the hot seat and be 'forced' to listen while other members were invited to say what they most appreciated about what the person brought to the team. It didn't take long to realize that we were going to be there awhile. It took three hours to get through our entire team. Not everyone spoke every time— only those who genuinely had something to say. I'm not usually the 'touchy-feely' type, but when facades dropped and people got real, it was just too good not to enjoy. That will always stand as one of the most memorable events of my life, because it is a rare occasion in anyone's life to be on either the giving or receiving end of such a quality time of recognizing what people contribute."

What kind of manager can make employees who aren't the "touchy-feely" type comfortable with a recognition event that resembles an encounter group? When I interviewed Boyes, I learned that she was a retired army first sergeant who has been awarded numerous prestigious leadership awards. Her background provided plenty of experience with formal recognition programs. Clearly, she also had the opportunity to learn how to give the kind of personalized recognition that Wheeler described.

Boyes told me that Williams doesn't have an enterprise-wide recognition program. So far, recognition has been left up to individual managers. This works as an overall strategy, but only if the manager has a good grasp on what makes recognition effective. Clearly, Boyes is a manager who understands what makes employees feel recognized. She offers these tips to help you offer recognition that works:

Tip #1: Provide clear expectations, validation, respect, loyalty, and trust. Boyes focuses on building strong working relationships with each person because she knows this is the foundation for effective recognition.

Tip #2: Figure out what people have to offer and leverage those strengths. According to Boyes, the key to making people feel recognized is to select challenges and opportunities that are appropriate for and stretch the individual while still focusing on results.

Tip #3: Individualize recognition. Boyes makes sure she knows enough about employees to select recognition that they will value. Individualizing recognition was the key to making the "hot seat" so successful. She knew her team well enough to know that, even with initial reluctance, they would warm up to the idea of taking turns recognizing each other verbally. She uses this same knowledge about what her people value to select recognition awards when appropriate.

Tip #4: Encourage employees to recognize each other. The recognition session at their retreat was only one example of peers recognizing each other. Team members acknowledge each other regularly—whenever they see someone doing something right. Boyes encourages her employees by modeling good behavior and coaching them to be alert for opportunities to recognize each other.

Tip #5: Celebrate as a team. Once a year they have a formal recognition event for the team. Three volunteers put a dinner together that includes some form of fun recognition activity for the group.

Company #2

Another response to my request for the names of managers with exceptional recognition skills came from Bruno Petrauskas. He submitted the name of a manager he had worked for eleven years earlier! Elizabeth Dressner was Petrauskas's manager when he worked as a technical writer for Information Associates, an IT solution provider based in Rochester, New York. Dressner managed his group of twenty-four technical writers. According to Petrauskas,

"She was my manager for several years, and she was truly exceptional at making me feel valued, appreciated, and recognized."

It had been eleven years since Petrauskas worked for Dressner, yet when faced with the question of exceptional recognition, her name came to mind immediately. How did Dressner create that kind of impact? According to Petrauskas, it was mostly the little things. It was regular gestures of appreciation, "When I would get a 'praise and thanks-for-your-contribution' e-mail from someone, Elizabeth would send me a note to express her own appreciation and praise and then forward both the e-mail and her note to her own manager and the personnel department." She demonstrated to Petrauskas how much she valued having him as a part of her team. "There were a number of times that we had to work extra long hours to get a particular job or project done. One time I had already put in over fifty hours by the middle of the week. I recall Elizabeth coming to my cubicle, taking one look at me (I did look tired and beat), and telling me to go home immediately and rest, not just for that day but the next as well. She really cared about my well-being."

When I interviewed Dressner, I learned that Information Associates had formal recognition programs and that her current company has its programs as well. In Dressner's experience, formal programs don't work that well, regardless of the company. She says they never seem to hit the mark and sometimes even have the opposite result.

Recently, her current employer asked Dressner to be part of a team that is evaluating their formal recognition programs. According to Dressner, the team's preliminary findings confirm that "the efforts of managers are far more effective in terms of employee morale and satisfaction" than are the formal programs that they have in place. She believes, "You can't rely on anyone else to give your folks the recognition that they need."

What tips does Dressner offer on how to make people feel recognized?

Tip #1: Make recognition personal. Face to face, Dressner tells people they are doing a great job and that their team wouldn't accomplish what it does without their help. Petrauskas shared that a good reward for him was time off. Dressner helped him to accumulate time off in exchange for overtime hours. The arrangement helped them bring projects in on time and allowed Petrauskas to supplement his vacation time for a longer trip. For others, recognition may be time off to do their holiday shopping, tickets to a movie or sporting event, or a certificate for merchandise at the company store or dinner out. Employee preferences help Dressner choose what is appropriate.

Tip #2: Stay available and visible. Dressner's door is always open, and if she is in her office, employees are always welcome. Much of the time, though, she is out of the office talking with employees.

Tip #3: Arrange departmental recognition events. Dressner's team has regular celebrations, such as lunches a couple of times a month and parties for new software releases. They held their own Academy Awards where everyone received an award. These awards took into account each person's unique role on the team. They presented one person with a pair of handmade gold lamé gloves, "The Golden Fingers Award," because this person had completed a huge typing project without a single typographical error. Another, a team leader, received an oilcan for "oiling the sticky parts of the corporate bureaucracy."

Tip #4: Encourage your team to become involved in community outreach activities. Dressner's team plans and sponsors events that benefit charities. They participate in walkathons. They serve lunch and officiate over bingo games at a nearby senior center. These activities improve team spirit, and the community recognizes and appreciates their efforts.

Company #3

Deb Tacker, an employee at Remedy, the software company mentioned in the introduction, nominated the third manager included in this chapter. Tacker works in a different department, but she had observed that Janet Lewis, a support services manager of sixteen people on two technical support teams, did an excellent job of recognizing her people. Subsequent interviews with two of Lewis's direct reports, both technical support engineers, confirmed Tacker's observations. Valerie Ford told me that Lewis "goes out of her way to recognize the little things. You don't have to save a big account in order to hear from her." Lisa Murray shared that Lewis "recognizes my capabilities even more than I do myself. She talks with me about where I am and where I want to be. She points out strengths and makes suggestions for new directions."

Remedy Support Services does an excellent job of recognizing employees. Lewis confesses that, at their location, things can get a little zany. Employees get regular visits from the Cookie Lady, who comes to their offices and bakes fresh cookies. There is an Employee Appreciation Week as well as quarterly campaigns tied to fun themes and goals. One campaign to raise customer survey scores to a level that many managers had doubted was possible ended with a chicken-themed celebration ("Management was 'chicken,' but we knew we could do it!"), complete with chicken barbecue, egg drop contest, and a presentation where the managers did the chicken dance. To top it off, their VP, Mike Little, now also affectionately known as Chicken Little, dressed up in a chicken costume. These kinds of activities won't fit into every organization's culture, but the people in Remedy Support Services think they are a perfect fit and say they offer a solid foundation for the recognition that managers offer.

What does a manager do, in an atmosphere such as this, to make their direct reports feel even more valued? In Lewis's case, she does many of the same things as the other managers described in this chapter. Lewis makes a point of remembering that what motivates one person won't necessarily motivate another. Like Boyes, she provides challenges that are achievable but at the same time provide an opportunity for growth. Like Dressner, she makes herself available and provides focused attention.

Lewis also encourages employees to create their own recognition. One of her direct reports came up with an idea for peer recognition. Michael Fahrenbruch felt that the engineers knew better than anyone else the achievements their peers had made, and he suggested a program he called "Kudos for Kolleagues." Lewis was enthusiastic, so when another engineer wanted to develop the idea and work with her peers to set the criteria and implement the program, Lewis encouraged her. Now engineers use Kudos for Kolleagues to recognize each other for a variety of things, from helping them fix their telephone headset to volunteering to take the early shift.

Lewis makes the following suggestions on how you can provide valued recognition:

Tip #1: Give instant feedback. When Lewis gets positive feedback about an employee, she adds her positive comments and forwards both to the employee. She says that "little recognition" means as much or more than "big recognition."

Tip #2: Engineer "easy wins." This doesn't mean give employees easy tasks. Provide achievable challenges that people are passionate about delivering. Then give them the help that they need in order to deliver.

Tip #3: Motivate the team to recognize each other. Lewis asks her teams to set quarterly goals for the number of Kudos for Kolleagues that they will give each other. She says they never have trouble exceeding that goal.

Tip #4: Hold one-on-one meetings. Lewis does this with every employee each quarter. She makes a point of telling top performers that their contribution is key. She says it's important that these people know that you don't take them for granted.

Recognition Doesn't Require Organizational Support

There are no big secrets to what you, as a manager or supervisor, can do to make employees feel recognized. It comes down to the basics of really knowing the people who work for you, challenging them to do their best, and then recognizing them for their achievements. It is easier when your organization supports your recognition efforts. But if they don't, still do the same things, and you'll still have a positive impact. Without organizational support, you will most likely have to work within a very limited budget, but as the examples have shown, effective recognition doesn't necessarily require a lot of money.

By paying attention to recognition preferences, offering flexibility and opportunity, giving praise and celebrating both individual and team success, you can significantly increase the job satisfaction of the people who work for you. When you begin to get results, both in terms of higher employee retention and increased productivity, you will most likely find that senior management will be more supportive and willing to budget for recognition.

Even if the organization never supports your recognition efforts, you will still be effective if you focus on the basics. To quote one employee who was asked who he wanted recognition from, "My vote is still with the line supervisor or manager who brings in a case of pop at break time on a hot day . . . that's a tough act for any organization to beat."

TAKING ACTION

- Keep it simple. You can begin by recognizing both the individuals and teams who work directly for you and by acknowledging others when their work affects your group. Offer thanks and praise. Send e-mails, mention results face to face, and send a hand-written note occasionally. Look for ways to increase inherent recognition. Develop people by providing appropriate opportunities. Demonstrate that your employees are a valued part of your team.

- Be consistent. Offer equivalent recognition for similar achievements. Consistency doesn't mean you always have to give the same recognition. To be fair, recognition doesn't have to be the same, just of similar value. The three managers described in this chapter show that it is important to respect individual preferences. Consistency also doesn't mean that people have to be achieving at exactly the same level in order to be recognized; they simply need to be making progress.

- Keep it coming. Frequent recognition is more important than grand gestures. Employees said that recognition from managers was about the everyday little things that the manager did to demonstrate the employees' value to them. To get into the habit of offering frequent recognition, start by finding something positive to recognize about each person at least once each month. As you become more proficient, work toward making sure that your people are recognized at least once per week.

- Reassess your role in the recognition process. Learn more about what you can do to improve recognition. The next few chapters are focused on the roles that others play in recognition that works. Even though these chapters address what other people in your organization should be doing in order to offer more effective recognition, you will find ideas that will help you as well.

chapter 5

Leaders Provide Vision, Visibility, and Momentum

Leaders play a unique role in the recognition process. Just as they determine the direction of an organization, they can determine the direction that recognition takes. Typically, the visibility and influence of the executive team makes them the most effective proponents of recognition within their organization. From their small, personal gestures, to the recognition programs that they personally champion, the members of the executive team set the tone for recognition. If the leadership values recognition, then it's much more likely that everyone within the organization will value it as well. Members of the executive team are in the best position to weave recognition into the fiber of the organization. To better understand exactly how an effective leader does this, let's look at a few examples.

Developing a Culture of Inherent Recognition

Some leaders focus on the recognition that is inherent in the workplace, working to ensure that their employees receive recognition directly from the work environment. They create an organizational culture focused on mutual respect, opportunity, and pride. This is true at Design Octaves, Inc., a small manufacturing firm with less than one hundred employees. I have consulted with Design Octaves for a number of years and have observed firsthand how Norm Weiss, company president, ensures that his employees feel recognized.

Design Octaves has only one formal recognition program. After ten years of service, Weiss recognizes employees with a trip to Hawaii. At one time, the company also had an employee of the month award, but Weiss chose to discontinue it. Instead, he spends his time ensuring that employees feel valued and respected.

When I first began consulting with Design Octaves, something happened that clearly illustrated that powerful recognition can come simply from the way employees are treated. I was brought into Design Octaves to oversee a project that typically would take a few months to complete. I observed that employees throughout the company were upbeat, loyal, hardworking, and productive. I took this as a good sign. Employees with this kind of positive attitude and commitment would help ensure that the project would go smoothly, and we would finish quickly.

It wasn't long before I knew that the project I had been hired to oversee would become one of the longer and more time-consuming projects I had ever done. It wasn't that the project itself was anything out of the ordinary or that the people weren't motivated. The lack of productivity occurred because the people on my team had absolutely no experience in doing the kind of work that we were asked to do. The lack of experienced team members quickly made this an expensive project for the client.

What happened next showed me how powerful inherent recognition can be. When I went to Weiss and described the problem,

I expected that he would want to hire someone with experience to join this team. That would have been the most cost-effective solution. So I was surprised to discover that Weiss was already aware that we were proceeding at a fraction of the pace of a more experienced team. That was all right with him. He was more than willing to pay the extra money in order to train the existing team. He believed that his people were worth investing in. The employees on this team knew he had cheaper options, and they knew he was committed to their growth.

Knowing the level of commitment Weiss had to them, these employees felt the same kind of commitment to him. They knew that what he offered was real recognition. It was recognition that said, "You are important," "What you do is important to me," and "I will help you become even more important to the company by providing you with new opportunities." The money Weiss spent to train members of his "family," when he clearly could have recruited more qualified people, had a lasting impact on these employees.

Not much has changed at Design Octaves over the years. Every morning Weiss grabs a cup of coffee and then heads out to the factory floor. He hugs people, shakes their hands, and calls them by name. He says, "I try to make some sort of contact with every person every day. They know that I'm there, that I see them, and that I recognize them." The respect Weiss shows employees sets the tone throughout the organization. He models what recognition at Design Octaves should look like, and employees follow his lead. Everyone is highly respectful of everyone else, and they all look for ways to assist each other. They recognize the value of every member of their team and work together to provide the kind of workplace where commitment and loyalty are prevalent and turnover is less than 2 percent a year.

Weiss provides leadership by modeling a recognition strategy that focuses on mutual respect. He sets the tone for a company culture that offers inherent recognition. Compare that to this food-processing company, as described by a former employee:

"I worked at a company that was outwardly hip and socially responsible. They talked about shared goals and values. We created mission, vision, and values in a series of company-wide meetings. We were told that we were responsible for keeping the company true to our values and goals. But it was a crazy-making situation because upper management repeatedly violated core values and failed to provide the resources to implement very important goals around safety, working conditions, and customer complaints."

It seemed as though the leaders of this organization wanted to create a workplace that provided inherent recognition. They told employees they were responsible for creating their own environment. If employees had been able to create their own environment, they would have felt recognized for their trustworthiness, competency, and ability to direct themselves. Instead, when the executive team sabotaged their efforts every step of the way, they felt betrayed. Unfortunately, this happens in far too many organizations. The members of the executive team generally know what needs to happen and say the words that they know employees want to hear, but then, through their actions, demonstrate that they really didn't mean what they said.

Showing Value Through Action

What the executive team truly believes about recognition comes through, first and foremost, in its actions. Do the executives take a hands-off approach and decide that recognition is someone else's responsibility? Do they declare that recognition needs to happen and then stand back and wait? Or do they roll up their sleeves and lead the way with their own actions? The more willing the executive team is to get involved, the more employees see their leaders' commitment to recognition.

In a workshop years ago, a manager told this story:

"I travel a lot, and consequently have experienced a lot of flight delays. During a delay on American Airlines, I got to talking to the passenger seated next to me. It turned out that the guy worked for American Airlines and was somehow involved in the repair of the planes. He went on to tell me that the last time he was on a delayed flight, the cause of the delay was fuel leaking from the jet. After a flight crew (not American Airlines) examined the plane, they determined that it required a part that would take four hours to arrive. Four hours. This was the only flight out that day, and a four-hour delay would cause nearly everyone on board to miss connecting flights. The captain came back to ask this off-duty employee if he would please check out the problem. Even though he was dressed in a suit, he went to check it out. Soon he discovered that the problem was a simple gasket. It was quickly fixed, and the flight was on its way.

The airline employee didn't tell me this just to brag about how dedicated he was. Rather he was impressed by something else. It turned out that the pilot had sent a letter to the president of American Airlines. The president then sent a letter to the employee, thanking him for his dedication and extending a personal invitation. The employee seated next to me, telling me his story, was now on his way to have dinner with the president and his wife."

Because of their visibility, leaders are in an excellent position to model how important recognition is. When managers and employees see the presidents and vice presidents of their organizations recognizing people, they're more inclined to see the value in offering recognition and are more likely to offer it themselves. Also, gestures of recognition that come from the leadership of an organization can have a very big impact, no matter how small the gesture. Being noticed by top-level management is often especially powerful. When I asked employees about recognition that had made their day, several described a time when their vice president stopped by their cubicle to chat. During their conversations, each of these employees discovered that the VP knew something about the work they were doing. That simple awareness was meaningful recognition. It was powerful because most employees, especially in larger organizations, don't expect personal attention from the executive team.

Griffin Health, the fastest growing hospital in Connecticut, offers another example of the power of personal attention from the executive team. The CEO, Vice President, and VP of Patient Care Services oversee a daylong orientation for new employees and volunteers. The day is crammed full of valuable information about the hospital and its service philosophy. When the executive team began doing this orientation, they expected that the knowledge that employees and volunteers gained would be what they valued most. Instead, when asked, employees and volunteers said that what they valued most about the orientation was "that the three senior executives spent the day with us." Wendy Silver, R.N., went through a recent orientation and said, "I was impressed that the CEO spoke for two hours about the hospital's values and customer service focus to educate new employees." Deborah Gibber, a new Quality Manager said, "I felt truly welcomed and valued." Employees and volunteers know that the executives' time is limited, and they are impressed that this team would choose to spend the day sharing information and getting to know them. The people who work at Griffin Health know they are important from the moment they are hired.

Personal attention from the executive team can be powerful, but the leadership at Griffin Health knows that recognition needs to come from many different fronts. Although they don't really think of it this way, they have worked to create an environment that contains inherent recognition. Griffin Health has a terrific reputation and is best known for its remarkable, almost fanatical customer service. The service is so exceptional that, to date, more than four hundred hospitals have visited Griffin Health in order to learn more about how they do it. The hospital's reputation offers significant inherent recognition. Employees have a tremendous amount of pride in the quality of their service. The exceptional level of customer service is also significant because when customers feel important, it's a good indicator that employees also feel important. Quality service rarely comes from employees who feel undervalued. The environment at Griffin Health attracts the best people in their industry. Top physicians want to work there, and the hospital has a low turnover among its nurses—something that is almost unheard of in the healthcare industry.

Leading Organization-Wide Recognition Efforts

The leadership of Griffin Health knows that inherent recognition alone is not enough. When recent surveys showed that recognition from managers was below standards, the executive team took ownership of the problem. They presented each manager with a recognition toolbox. This was an actual toolbox filled with gift certificates, videos, and more. Managers are expected to use the box as a resource for offering on-the-spot recognition to their employees. There hasn't been a follow-up survey yet, but according to Bill Powanda, Vice President, "based on the number of times we have had to refill the boxes, it's going well." Most managers quickly adopted the idea of spot recognition and used the toolbox to reward their people. Because the idea came from the executive team, managers knew that implementation was a priority.

Most organizations make the human resources group responsible for rolling out recognition programs and providing training to managers on effective recognition techniques. They expect this group to create successful recognition without the assistance of the leadership. While the people in HR can do a great job developing

the structure, it is nearly impossible for them to excite and motivate people to participate without a champion from the executive
team. Organization-wide recognition must be led. When there is
commitment from the leadership, it tells the rest of the organization, "This is important. Make it work."

Among their many responsibilities, the executive team is generally responsible for keeping the organization's values in front of
employees. This is true whether the leadership realizes it or not.
Employees listen not only to the words they speak but also to the
actions they take.

> "From the outset, my old CEO talked a good game. He
> wanted a culture based on trust, respect, learning, and
> open communication. Unfortunately, he couldn't see how
> his denigrating approach to managing performance (berat-
> ing, belittling) shut us down. He was all for open feed-
> back—so long as it was positive feedback. He wanted
> people to trust him, but he played games with the com-
> pensation packages. People just couldn't take him at his
> word anymore."

Leaders who state the organizational values, mission, and
strategic plan on a regular basis and then demonstrate through
their actions that they believe in these things, send a powerful,
congruent message to employees. One of the best ways to reinforce
that message is with recognition. John Mitchell, VP of Engineering at Pella Windows & Doors, believes in this philosophy. He
sees value in Pella's recognition programs, such as Moment of
Truth and Successful Teamwork Achieving Results (STAR), both
employee-nominated awards.

Mitchell's approach to recognition isn't warm and fuzzy. He
isn't focused on making employees feel good, and he rarely thinks
about recognition as an end in itself. When asked about a traveling trophy award that he instituted last year, he said, "It grew

more out of a desire to reinforce or recognize innovation than 'how do I reward employees?'" Mitchell's goal was to produce results.

Engineering already held a quarterly meeting where teams reported on how they were doing. Mitchell decided that it was the perfect forum to reinforce the importance of innovation. Now, each quarter, he asks the teams to prepare a presentation describing their most innovative idea of that quarter. As the teams make their presentations, senior management rates each idea. Before the meeting ends, the scores are tallied and the trophy, a twelve-inch version of a Pella window, is presented to the winning team. They get to display the trophy until the next meeting when new innovative ideas are presented.

Many ideas are generated by the contest. Some are particularly noteworthy. A couple of years ago the Patio Door product team proposed the Patio Door Rolscreen, a screen that nearly disappears into the door casing when it's not in use. Building off the company's existing technology for casement windows, the team applied the Rolscreen idea to patio doors.

The contest itself and the recognition that comes from receiving the trophy put the focus on innovation. Mitchell says, "People think the Innovative Idea Contest is a lot of fun. Even though many of the ideas will never see the light of day, it creates a lot of energy and spurs further idea generation."

Part of leadership is defining and reinforcing mission, values, and strategic plans. But leaders can't just tell people what is important and expect it to stick. They need to find ways to reinforce what is valued. Recognition can do that—with the support of leadership. When the executive team champions a recognition program, they give it credibility and visibility. When they personally offer effective recognition, they model it for everyone within the organization. By their words and actions, leaders can have a profound impact on recognition and, in turn, on the success of their organization.

TAKING ACTION

Leaders

- Focus on creating inherent workplace recognition. Demonstrate that you respect and value employees and the contributions they make.
- Get to know as many employees as possible. Talk to them frequently. Your interest in your employees' personal and professional lives is real recognition.
- Model good recognition habits. Managers, supervisors, and employees will follow your lead.
- Cheer the recognition efforts of your managers. Take the lead on any programs your organization rolls out. It's up to you to generate excitement and commitment.

Managers

- Leadership isn't a title. It's a way of behaving. As a manager or supervisor, you can do most of what is described in this chapter, just on a smaller scale than the executive team. Every Taking Action item directed at leaders applies to you as well. Model good recognition habits for your employees. Cheer their efforts at recognizing each other. Create inherent recognition. Take the lead.

Human Resources— Best Department in a Supporting Role

Why a Supporting Role?

Every spring the Academy of Motion Picture Arts and Sciences gives out the awards known as the Oscars. Other than Best Picture, the awards that create the most excitement and get the most media attention are Best Actor and Best Actress. The actors and actresses nominated for these awards are Hollywood's stars, but the Academy knows these people can't do it alone. They also give out awards for director, sound, special effects, editing, and more. The people who receive these awards are highly respected professionals with vitally important roles in the process of creating great movies. Without their support, films would never get made and the stars would never shine.

Employee recognition also has starring and supporting roles and, as with the Oscars, both types of roles are vitally important. Because the relationships people have with each other determine whether or not recognition works, the stars of employee recognition are the people being recognized and the people whose businesses, lives, and jobs they impact. A manager recognizes a team that has accomplished its objective. An employee recognizes his or her supervisor for providing needed support. A vice president recognizes a division for meeting a goal. Managers, supervisors, teams, and individual employees—these people are the stars of recognition that works.

In the best organizations, Human Resources plays a highly successful role in the recognition process. In these organizations, management is responsible for recognition while Human Resources guides and supports them, remaining behind the scenes, influencing and coaching both senior executives and managers rather than trying to lead.

Organizations fail at recognition when they make the mistake of asking Human Resources to play a starring role in the process. Any department that administers or facilitates the employee recognition process (we will refer to them as Human Resources or HR) will be much more effective in a supporting role. Meaningful recognition must come from someone affected by the recognized behavior or achievement. Recognition that comes from HR lacks the personal touch and relevance necessary to make it effective. Imagine yourself receiving administered recognition:

Your HR department arranges for every employee to receive a potted plant on the anniversary of his or her hire date. The computer generates a list of employees with upcoming anniversaries, an HR employee creates the purchase order, and a florist delivers your plant. When your manager walks by your desk and notices that you have received the standard anniversary plant, she says, "Oh, is it your anniversary?" At that moment, how recognized do you feel? Does it matter to you that the people in HR know it's your anniversary? Unless you have a relationship with HR, it probably doesn't. For most people, this kind of recognition has about as much value as a computer-generated birthday greeting from their life insurance company.

Recognition only has meaning when it comes from people who benefit from your behavior or have a direct interest in your achievements. Anything else is cold, impersonal, and a waste of company resources. To turn around the anniversary plant idea, HR needs to step out of the starring role and into a supporting or facilitating role. The department can still generate the anniversary list and order the plants, but their representative should deliver the plant and the name of the employee directly to the manager. The department might take it a step further and provide an anniversary card. After that, it is up to the manager to prepare a personal note and deliver the plant. The manager's actions will determine whether or not the anniversary gift makes a positive impression, because it's the interaction between the employee and manager, and not the plant itself, which is meaningful.

Recognition Is Not a Function of Human Resources

When the people in HR discover that job satisfaction is suffering because employees crave recognition, they can find themselves in a frustrating position. They have identified a need, and they want to do something to correct the problem. If management ignores the problem, often HR will take the lead. They create sophisticated and imaginative programs, survey employees on preferences, create metrics, and track results. In many cases, they have an excellent understanding of the mechanics of recognition. While their intentions are admirable, inevitably, when they take the lead, they fail.

Even if HR has support from the organization's leaders, their recognition efforts can still fail. Consider the CEO who approaches the Director of Human Resources and asks him to create and implement a recognition program. The CEO provides the budget and then leaves it in his capable hands. The director designs a great program, announces it to the employees and their managers, and after a few months of unenthusiastic response, the CEO either says that it was the wrong program or that recognition doesn't work. Neither would be true. The problem is the perception that it is HR's program and not the CEO's program. HR has stepped out of the supporting role. Once HR designs the program, they need to give ownership back to the CEO and let the CEO announce and lead the program.

What HR Does Best

So what does it mean to have a supporting role? It means doing most of the work while taking little of the credit. But it can also mean contributing in a meaningful way to a very successful program and adding considerable value to management's recognition efforts. HR can significantly improve the recognition process and employee job satisfaction. Here are some tips on how to do that.

Tip #1: Survey the managers in order to discover their knowledge and attitudes regarding recognition. The executive team can use this information to predict which managers will be most effective at recognizing employees and which will need training or coaching.

Tip #2: Survey the employees to learn their current level of job satisfaction. If administrators also identify departments or divisions for each survey participant, they can pinpoint where recognition is working and where it isn't. The executive team can use this information to make decisions that impact job satisfaction.

Tip #3: Offer or recommend training or coaching on how to provide meaningful recognition. Managers should view training and coaching as valuable resources for their use. If they will be required to attend training or receive coaching in order to correct a deficiency, the executive team, not HR, should mandate it.

Tip #4: Help management provide more variety. Design programs such as employee-nominated peer recognition awards. Coordinate celebratory events that improve employee interaction and job satisfaction. Provide reward ideas.

Tip #5: Track program results and provide feedback to managers. You can help managers see their progress by providing the necessary metrics. *See* chapters 10 and 12 for more on this.

As you can see, HR can provide services that play a pivotal role in the recognition process. The expertise this department provides is often crucial. HR can have the biggest role in employee recognition—it just works best if that role is behind the scenes.

The Supporting Role in Action

FedEx Freight understands recognition. Walk into the lobby or down any hall of its West Coast offices and you will find dozens of awards for outstanding performance, most given to them by their customers. It's evident, in the hundreds of plaques on display throughout the building, that employees are proud of the excellent job they do for their customers and appreciate the recognition they receive.

FedEx Freight knows the value of recognition and demonstrates that knowledge to its employees with the many recognition opportunities it provides. Programs include truck-driving championships where drivers compete to be the best driver in the country, and employee-nominated awards for being "Easy To Do Business With" (EZTDBW) and generating additional revenue (the Moment of Truth Award). Managers and directors give awards for safety and performance. There is a company-wide celebration known as

Employee Appreciation Week. In each of these programs, the people in Human Resources play an active and vital role. They work to make employee recognition more effective.

One of HR's most important functions is to track what works and what doesn't and use this knowledge to recommend effective changes. Tom Suchevits, Vice President of Human Resources at FedEx Freight West, said that when his department looked at the Service Center of the Year Award (based on hours between injuries, miles between accidents, on-time performance, and other factors), they determined that the award didn't provide enough opportunities for recognition. Suchevits recommended they change it to the Service Center of the Quarter Award, giving four times more opportunity for recognition. He also recommended a change in the award itself—originally a dinner dance for everyone at the service center, now they award a cash prize that each service center uses to celebrate as they choose. What do the employees of the service centers choose? Some still choose dinners. Others take a weekend trip together, raffle off large prizes, have a barbecue, or provide each employee with a gift card from a local store. Each celebrates in a way that makes sense to them.

To figure out what is working and what isn't, FedEx Freight's HR department administers two surveys, the Quality of Worklife Survey (the complete QOWL survey appears in chapter 12) and the Workplace Employee Satisfaction Survey (WESS). The QOWL Survey includes twenty-four questions, and everyone throughout the company gets the opportunity to complete it. Most employees gather in their facility's break room to complete the survey. Those who are out of the office when the survey is administered get a copy in their mailbox. They have an excellent return rate of 77 percent (2001), although not as good as they would like. Human Resources is working to find ways to improve that return rate and get a 100 percent return.

The QOWL survey identifies the service center, location, department, and job function of each respondent. One purpose of the survey is to offer insight into which managers and supervisors are most effective. The challenge is to be able to offer this kind of information while keeping respondent identities anonymous. Only in an anonymous survey will people be truly honest in their evaluation. Respondents would have better anonymity if they didn't identify location, department, or job function, but HR believes the improved ability to determine both the effectiveness of employee recognition programs and the effectiveness of managers and supervisors offsets that loss.

Frustrated by minimal improvement in the QOWL survey each year, Human Resources at FedEx Freight recommended the administration of a second annual survey, the Workplace Employee Satisfaction Survey (WESS). The questions on the WESS are very similar to the QOWL; the difference lies in the administration. A member of the HR team travels to each facility and gives the survey to all the employees at that location. This time employee answers are not anonymous. While still on-site, the team analyzes the results and compiles a list of the negative responses. They use the list to meet individually with those employees who gave low scores. For instance, at one facility, the statement "Work rules and policies are fair," received a number of poor marks from the drivers. When the HR representative interviewed the drivers, he discovered that a driver had been penalized for an accident the other drivers considered unavoidable. In their view, the driver was not at fault; therefore the policy was unfair. HR provided the results of these interviews to the director of the local facility. The director met with the facility manager to discuss the results and create an action plan for resolving the issues that were uncovered. Knowing the underlying causes of poor scores and using that information to make meaningful changes will improve survey results and employee job satisfaction.

FedEx Freight also offers training on their recognition programs. The executive team wants to do what they can to ensure all managers and supervisors are knowledgeable and enthusiastic about every recognition program the company offers. Once a year they review, with their managers, how each program works and what impact it has had on employees and the organization.

When asked about FedEx Freight's success with job satisfaction and the role Human Resources plays, Suchevits said, "HR's role is about process." As an example, he noted the QOWL survey process: Each year HR administers the survey, analyzes the results, and recommends a time line for creating an action plan and reporting the information to employees. The department provides tabulated survey results to the service center managers, along with talking points for sharing the information in an employee meeting. Directors work with their managers to address the results of the survey.

The company is looking for long-term results and improvement. It wants long-term commitment from everyone. Neither the executive team nor the managers are interested in "flavor of the month" recognition. Long-term commitment is what makes FedEx Freight's recognition successful. EZTDBW is not just a slogan it is a way of life, and Human Resources offers excellent support for the process.

Success in a Supporting Role

As FedEx Freight shows, Human Resources can have a very active and successful role in its organization's recognition efforts. Some of the ways HR can most appropriately facilitate the process are to help establish program structure, survey employees and managers, and provide information and guidance to the executive team. Given the appropriate budget and management support, HR can be a very successful part of management's recognition team.

TAKING ACTION

Recognition Program Administrators

- Make sure that the executive team supports your efforts. The executive team needs to take the leading role in promoting the value of recognition. They need to create buy-in among managers. HR can uncover poor attitudes and lack of understanding, but only the top management can act to correct them.
- Don't force a recognition program on reluctant managers. You are better off focusing on managers and supervisors who are enthusiastic. Even with only one manager's or supervisor's buy-in, you can have a successful pilot program. If you let that manager lead the program, you can demonstrate success that the executive team can use to showcase the program to other managers.
- Make sure managers are knowledgeable. Good intentions are not enough. Don't roll out a new program to managers who don't understand recognition basics. Without that understanding, it's common for managers to not only be ineffective but to actually damage morale. It is your responsibility to find and report shortcomings to the leadership. Offer recommendations for workable solutions, and then let them recommend or require training, coaching, or whatever will be most effective.

Managers

- Take advantage of the information HR gathers. If they survey employees and track departments, you will find the information that they can provide will help you be more effective at offering recognition that works.

- Take the lead on HR's recognition efforts within your department. HR makes your job easier by handling the logistics of more complicated recognition programs. Take ownership of the programs they develop and make them successful within your department. If you do, you will add variety to the kinds of recognition you offer employees.

chapter 7

Recognition Is the Responsibility of Every Employee

Catching the Recognition Bug

When a person with a cold enters a room and sneezes or coughs, everyone is potentially exposed to the germs. Within a short amount of time, many of those exposed will also become ill and spread the bug to even more people. Infect a computer with a virus, and soon computers around the world are infected. What starts with just one person or one computer soon infiltrates whole communities. The impact of the virus expands exponentially.

We know all about viruses and go out of our way not to catch them. When we can, we immunize ourselves or take precautions to avoid catching a bug and getting sick. We have software programs designed to protect our computers from viruses. We're careful because we know viruses, in any form, are invasive and can quickly spread. But let's look at catching a bug from a different point of view. What if a virus was a good thing, and we wanted it to spread? Imagine recognition as a virus and you as the carrier. You recognize a coworker for helping you meet a deadline. You feel good, and your coworker feels good. You both enjoy the warm feeling that comes from this positive experience. You both feel more generous, and so you each recognize someone else. Now four people feel recognized; they see their relationships with their coworkers more positively. Four people are now more inclined to recognize someone else. The recognition bug continues to spread. Before you know it, it can infect an entire organization, and it didn't have to start at the top. The infection can begin anywhere.

Taking the Initiative

In working with hundreds of burned-out and bored employees, I've found most share two beliefs. They believe their work environment is causing them to lose enthusiasm for their work. And they believe they have no control over that environment. In explaining their burnout, they describe bad bosses, uncooperative coworkers, rigid rules, and lack of communication. When I ask about recognition, inevitably they tell me that they don't get any. They tell me about managers and coworkers who are unappreciative of what they do.

When I ask if they give any recognition, they look at me like I have grown a second nose in the middle of my forehead; after all, we are talking about *their* burnout. The point they are missing is that people who get recognition are more likely to give it; that working in an environment where recognition is common predisposes people toward offering it themselves.

If you are part of an indifferent, recognition-free environment, you might feel reluctant to be the first person to offer recognition. This is understandable. When you offer recognition you acknowledge that other people contribute to your success. You have to be willing to share the credit for your accomplishments, and when you're barely receiving any recognition it is difficult to share. Do it anyway because, ultimately, the recognition you offer others will improve your work environment and increase the quantity and quality of recognition you receive in return.

Simple things make a difference, like writing a thank-you note to a coworker who covered for you when you had to leave early, or sending an e-mail to your boss telling him how much you appreciated the way he handled a problem you brought to his attention. If you want a more motivating work environment with greater levels of appreciation, take the initiative. Offer recognition to your boss and coworkers. Start spreading the virus. You will see an increase in the amount of appreciation everyone receives. You will improve your own job satisfaction and the satisfaction of everyone around you.

Peer Recognition

Peer recognition can be very powerful. It's easy to see how a workplace where employees show each other appreciation would be a more pleasant place to work. Employees in these organizations show each other greater respect and tend to act more cooperatively. Respect and cooperation create a more productive workplace, an obvious benefit for any organization.

Another benefit of creating a culture that focuses on peer recognition is that it increases the overall frequency of workplace recognition. In a department with twenty employees, a conscientious manager may recognize each employee once every other week. If employees in that department are in the habit of recognizing each other and each employee recognizes just four coworkers each month, the amount of recognition the average employee receives would nearly triple, significantly increasing the chances that each employee would feel adequately recognized.

Peer recognition can take three basic forms. It can be very unstructured and spontaneous, with employees simply acknowledging each other as they choose. It can be loosely structured, with the organization providing the awards and some criteria but letting employees decide when and how to give them. It can also be more formally structured, with systems in place for selecting recipients and managing the entire process.

Wells Fargo Bank's Internet Services Group, the division that handles all on-line banking, offers a good example of an organization that uses a variety of peer recognition options.

According to Jean Bourne, Senior Vice President of Human Resources, a survey of the Internet Services group's fifteen hundred employees revealed that only 50 percent of the employees were satisfied with the recognition they receive. When her department spoke with managers to see what could be done, their response was, "We are just moving so fast, we sometimes don't take the time to recognize everyone's contributions." Her team wanted to make it easy for everyone to provide recognition without significantly increasing anyone's workload, so they designed the E-wards program that they use today.

Their program consists of three parts:

1. *E-cards.* These are simple on-line cards that employees use to thank someone for something they have done. Anyone can give them to anyone else—anytime they choose. The e-card Web site guides givers through the process, asking questions and providing examples of how they might use the cards. The giver can copy the manager if he chooses. To increase excitement and program participation, another copy goes to a special recognition mailbox where cards are collected for a quarterly drawing for prizes. In the first year, employees sent sixteen hundred e-cards—a very good participation rate for year one.

2. *E-wards.* Instead of acknowledging a single incident, the intent of e-wards is to praise consistent performance over time. Anyone can complete an on-line form nominating anyone else.

The categories, based on what their group values, are leadership, e-novation, teams, entrepreneurship, and customer service. Employees can look at examples to get an idea of what the nomination should include. The e-wards nomination then goes to the nominee's manager for approval. The manager may return it to the person making the nomination for further clarification, because specific recognition is more effective than vague generalizations. Rarely is a nomination denied. After approval, the winner's manager gets three things: a certificate that details the nomination, a scratch-off ticket that will reveal a fifty- to two-hundred-dollar prize when it is scratched by the winner, and a sheet that provides ideas on how to present the award, depending on the recipient's preferences. The cost of the award is charged to the manager's unit, but they say the cost is minimal in comparison to a bonus or a day off. In 2001, employees presented more than nine hundred awards—another very good participation rate—with continued growth in 2002.

3. *Ride the Wave.* To create even more excitement for these two programs, once a year all e-card and e-ward recipients are eligible for inclusion in a special event. A committee of senior managers reviews the cards and nominations and selects seventy exemplary employees to attend a three-day off-site event with a guest of their choice. The event combines professional development with fun and a lot more recognition.

A follow-up survey didn't show the improvement that Bourne's group expected. The next step was to run focus groups to get to the source of the problem. Feedback showed that the programs are great. People love the peer recognition. At the same time they say that peer recognition doesn't replace the need for other forms of recognition. Many still want more direct recognition from their managers. They want their managers to use the program. They also want them to offer public praise, group recognition, and a simple "thanks—I appreciate your hard work." To get the kind of survey results Bourne's group wants, peer recognition is a great start—but it is only the beginning.

Informal Peer Recognition

When employees begin to acknowledge the people they work with, they have begun their own informal peer recognition program. They may be doing nothing more than thanking employees who assist them on projects or sending e-mails to the boss to describe how another employee helped them. Sandra Clark, a University of California Santa Cruz employee, told me about the drawer of kid's tools she has; it contains toy screwdrivers, hammers, and more. When someone in another department helps her "fix" something, anything from her computer to a personnel problem, she sends a tool and a "fix it" award thanking them for their help. It's not an organization-wide initiative; it's her way of showing appreciation. It's a simple courtesy that requires nothing of management and, over time, can positively affect the atmosphere of her workplace.

Peer recognition can be completely unstructured and left to the complete discretion of the employees. An organization can also take a slightly more organized approach to informal peer recognition, like Wells Fargo Bank's Internet group did with the e-card program. Typically, when an organization gets involved in informal peer recognition, they only provide the awards or prizes and some ideas about when they should be awarded. The rest is up to employees.

Many organizations use some kind of card or certificate that allows the giver to fill in the recipient's name and describe what they did that was noteworthy. I have seen "Star Bucks," "Caught in the Act," and "Brag Certificates." Regardless of what they are called, these cards offer a medium for thanks or praise. Usually, recipients can also redeem them at a later date for gifts or entry into some kind of a raffle.

Xilinx, the semiconductor company mentioned in chapter 3, gives each employee five "Values Medallions" each year. Employees give the medallions to those people who help them in some way and demonstrate the company's values of customer focus, respect, excellence, enjoying their work, accountability, teamwork, integrity, and communication. The giver of the medallion also provides the recipient with a very specific description of why they have received the medallion, reinforcing the valued behavior. The medallions have a Velcro tab so that employees can display them on their cubicles. They are on display throughout each building, and employees congratulate each other on having received one. The recipient's name is also entered into a drawing that takes place at the end of each quarter, offering further recognition for the valued behavior.

Don Peden, a manager at LSI Logic, another semiconductor company, helped his HR department through a difficult time by encouraging his people to develop their own informal recognition program. After a massive reduction in work force that had taxed their department's resources, they held a debrief session. In that session, Peden provided thank-you notes so that people could take a moment to show appreciation to anyone who had helped them through the process. Those notes ended up posted on bulletin boards and cubicle walls for several weeks afterward. By providing the supplies and a few minutes to write notes, Peden made it easier for employees to show their appreciation.

Nominations

Many companies use formal peer-nominated recognition systems. Done well, peer nomination can be a very effective recognition strategy. You saw one example with Wells Fargo's Internet group's e-ward program; Pella Windows & Doors does something similar. Employees recommend each other for "Moment of Truth" awards. The basis of Pella's "Moment of Truth" philosophy is the assumption that every decision and action by employees affects product value and the satisfaction customers receive. When employees see a coworker doing something above and beyond what is required, they submit that person's name for a Moment of Truth award. Managers review the recommendations but, as with Wells Fargo Bank's Internet group, most of the time they approve the award. The reward is small but highly valued—a Moment of Truth pen presented by the employee's manager and VP in front of their peers. Monthly recipients of the award are then mentioned in their internal publication.

Microsoft Great Plains Business Solutions, the division of Microsoft responsible for business management tools, gives another excellent example of how effective a structured peer-nominated recognition program can be. At Pioneer Days, the company's annual awards ceremony, they give out twelve different peer-nominated awards. Awards include the Sodbuster Award for overcoming obstacles, the Harvest Award for quality, the Jesse James Award for innovation, and the Eagle Award for leadership.

The Great Plains Human Resources Worklife Unit sends out a reminder of the criteria for each award. The unit also provides background on the purpose of each award and how it demonstrates what the company values. When the call for nominations goes out, employees and customers use the criteria to nominate the employees they feel are most deserving. Along with their nomination, they must provide a written description of why they believe a particular person deserves an award.

Anyone can nominate anyone else. Managers can nominate their own employees as well as employees from other departments. Employees can nominate their managers as well as their peers. A stock clerk is free to nominate the president and vice versa. Anyone who sees another person living the company values can nominate that person.

After the Worklife Unit receives the nominations, they sort through the responses and categorize them by award. For each award category, three people review the nominations and make recommendations. The reviewers include a past award recipient and a couple of senior leaders. The reviewers pass their recommendations on to the senior VPs who do the final review and select two to three recipients for each category. Then recipients are announced and the nomination letters are read at the Pioneer Days celebration.

What do employees think of the awards and what they represent?

"It was really rewarding to know that my peers thought I made a great contribution. The camaraderie and the congratulations that I received from fellow team members after the awards ceremony was extremely fulfilling."

—Chris Lerum, Manager, Tools and Technology Support

"I have received three different Pioneer Day Awards. They have all had one thing in common; each reaffirmed the fact that doing things differently is a good thing. I have always felt that by my receiving recognition for breaking the rules and asking hard questions, it has become okay for other folks to do so as well."

—Matt Gustafson, Program Manager

"Every time I attend Pioneer Day Awards and watch people I have met or worked with receive awards, listening to the great things they accomplish, and seeing some of their work personally, it always inspires me to do more and become better at what I do."

—Angela Hoy, Team Manager

"The great thing about the tradition of recognition at Great Plains is that it is consistent, fair, and diverse. People are recognized from all over the company for all kinds of good works, and I get to work with these people every day."

—Karl Gunderson, Software Design Engineer

"It was very rewarding to know that I made a difference, that my customers appreciated the services I provided to them. It motivated me to work even harder to provide the best customer service I can."

—JDee Muir, Print Service Specialist

Pioneer Days offer high-impact recognition because employees know what it takes to win each award. Someone reads each nomination letter during the presentation, providing a clear explanation of why a particular person received the award. The letters help to keep the program from becoming a popularity contest. They also reinforce the culture and values of the company by allowing employees to see examples of what is outstanding.

According to Mike Slette, Director of Human Resources, as powerful as the awards are, something just as powerful happens after the awards presentation. All nominees receive the letters that nominated them for an award. When they read the positive comments, they all feel like winners.

For anyone looking to set up a formal peer-nomination system:

- Develop clear nomination and selection criteria for each award.
- Have a nomination process that includes providing a description of what the person did to deserve the nomination.
- Allow for multiple recipients in order to acknowledge as many deserving people as possible.

What an Individual Can Do

What if your employer provides no structure for peer recognition? What can you do? Remember the recognition virus. Look for simple ways to acknowledge the efforts of the people you work with. Design and implement your own simple peer-recognition program, just as the university employee did with the tools. Be creative.

Some people give candy bars. The names of many candy bars lend themselves to recognition. You can give a Rocky Road™

candy bar to someone who has met a difficult challenge, a Three Musketeers™ for great teamwork, and a Milky Way™ to someone who has provided out-of-this-world customer service. Less common candies that work well include Panic Buttons™, Treasures™, and Dilbert Accomplish-Mints™. Use your imagination.

Small toys are also good. Use Silly Putty™ to recognize flexibility and creativity, or offer a Slinky™ in recognition of the ability to bounce back after being stretched to the limit. Again, your imagination can turn nearly any everyday object into a symbol of recognition.

If this type of recognition seems silly to you or, more important, would seem silly to the person you want to recognize, stick with a simple thank-you or praise for a job well-done. Give a card, send an e-mail, or tell them in person. After all, it's like your mother always said, "It's the thought that counts."

Recognizing Up

While you're at it, don't forget to recognize your manager or supervisor. Few people ever think to recognize up. Ask employees whom they recognize at work, and if they mention anyone, it would be subordinates and peers. Managers are the people employees bring problems to, not compliments. For many employees, acknowledging their manager in a positive way feels like "kissing up," "brown-nosing," or "apple-polishing," just to name a few of the slang terms used to show disdain for people who try to manipulate their managers with compliments.

How do you avoid being labeled a brown-noser? It is pretty simple really. First, recognize everyone, regardless of his or her ability to influence the direction of your career. If you recognize both your peers and your manager, your peers are less likely to think your being manipulative. Second, don't be manipulative. Be sincere. Don't offer recognition in order to get something. Do it to give something.

Managers appreciate recognition as much as the next person. Michelle Boyes, one of the managers mentioned in chapter 4, shared that a member of her team had nominated the team for a national award. Boyes felt honored that a member of the team thought their work was of award-winning caliber. For her, the greatest value was in the nomination by a team member. The award itself, while an honor, was less significant. When their team won the award, Boyes used the cash prize for a team celebration, bringing the recognition back full circle.

Most employees take good management for granted when they have it and complain loudly when they don't. If employees would recognize their managers and supervisors in a sincere manner, regardless of whether or not they currently receive any recognition from them, they would see a positive response. Just because some managers rarely give recognition doesn't mean they don't value it. More likely, they either feel under appreciated themselves or offering recognition simply hasn't occurred to them. In either case, employees who recognize their manager's efforts and accomplishments are more likely to receive recognition themselves.

Simple and Effective

Peer recognition is easy, and it works whether it is highly structured like Microsoft Great Plains Business Group's program, loosely structured like Xilinx's medallion program, or completely under individual control like the university employee's fix-it awards. Peer recognition improves employee relationships and the frequency of recognition.

Appreciation and acknowledgement are infectious. They spread from person to person like a virus and can change an entire organization. To develop a culture where peer recognition is the norm, the change can begin anywhere. With a little effort, anyone can have a significant impact on his or her own department. As we saw in the

Wells Fargo example, the change can even begin when a department makes the recognition process easier and adds a little excitement. Shift supervisor, filing clerk, technician, or team leader, regardless of where peer recognition begins, it can make a big impact and dramatically change the atmosphere of the workplace, resulting in higher productivity.

TAKING ACTION

Everyone Can

- Recognize everyone who has a positive impact. You don't have to be in a position of leadership to offer meaningful recognition. A sincere statement regarding the positive impact another person has had on you will always be valued.
- Use any existing peer recognition programs. Many companies encourage peer recognition by providing small gifts and opportunities to offer public recognition. If these are available, they can enhance the recognition you offer. If existing programs seem meaningless, add your own meaning.
- Take the initiative. Don't wait for someone to implement a program. Start your own. Find a way of recognizing others that suits you and your recipients. Use it frequently.

Self-Recognition— An Innovative Concept

Taking the Initiative

There is one company where the employees don't wait for someone else to make their day. They recognize themselves. They create scrapbooks filled with their accomplishments, along with photos, certificates, and letters from their customers. They prepare presentations to tell their coworkers about the dozens of improvements their team has made to operations. They take employees, managers, and the executive team on a hard-hat tour of a catwalk to show off a safety improvement they've made. Employees in this company take the initiative when it comes to recognizing themselves for the improvements they make.

What drives these employees to recognize themselves? Are they desperate for recognition? No. As a matter of fact, an internal job satisfaction survey at this company shows 81 percent overall employee satisfaction with the recognition that they receive for their contributions to the organization. Employees recognize themselves because their company values and promotes self-recognition.

Graniterock, a privately held, one-hundred-year-old company of around eight hundred employees, where the biggest recognition event is an opportunity for self-recognition, has made the *Fortune* list of the 100 Best Companies to Work For—not just once but four times. Their turnover rate is one-fifth of their industry average, 90 percent of their employees say it is a great place to work, and 88 percent plan to stay until they retire. Graniterock is clearly not a company that treats its employees poorly.

Graniterock employees get recognition. It takes many forms, from full-page ads thanking them for volunteering for community service to breakfast with the president and CEO Bruce Woolpert on their first day of work. Keith Severson, Marketing Services Manager at Graniterock, shared with me that when he had "Breakfast with Bruce," he sat next to another new employee, a cement-mixer truck driver. This driver told Severson that, in fifteen years on the job, he had never even met the president of his previous company. He was amazed to find that on his first day he was having breakfast with the president of Graniterock. This driver felt like an important part of the company. By simply having breakfast with these new-hires and showing that he is accessible, Woolpert recognizes the value of the people Graniterock hires. He offers recognition that works.

Leaders, managers, and coworkers at Graniterock do a good job of recognizing people. So why are they so proud of the recognition that they give themselves? The executive team believes that every employee is an entrepreneur, a leader within the organization. They don't refer to employees as employees, but as Graniterock People, and Graniterock People are expected to find problems and correct them. It is everyone's job to constantly improve the company and make sure that they receive acknowledgment for those improvements. Everyone is responsible for his or her own recognition. In fact, they have an obligation to share their accomplishments with their coworkers, and Graniterock has devised a program that helps them do this.

Recognition Days

The greatest opportunity for self-recognition at any Graniterock facility is Recognition Day. Each of the twenty-two northern California facilities hosts a Recognition Day once each year. Each facility schedules its Recognition Day on a different day in order to give employees the opportunity to attend as many of the twenty-two events as they can. Because Graniterock considers Recognition Days a learning experience, new employees are required to attend at least one each year for their first four years. Getting people to attend usually isn't a problem. The events are fun, unique, and informative.

Recognition Days always have an enthusiastic audience. Employees see their facility's Recognition Day as "their time," their opportunity to strut their stuff, not just in terms of their accomplishments, but also in terms of their creativity in putting together the event. Employees plan the event, choosing the theme and location. Groups have held their events on-site in order to show off recent innovations. They have also held them in more non-traditional locations. It is up to the volunteers who plan the event. To demonstrate safety improvements for working at night, they held one Recognition Day on the side of the freeway at 3:30 in the morning. Another was held at a shopping mall before it opened one morning, and two others were held at a miniature golf course and bowling alley where every hole or lane had a different presentation complete with review questions and prizes. Groups take advantage of the unique environment of each location in order to create excitement and reinforce the ideas they are presenting.

The presentations themselves are even more diverse than the locations employees select. People are free to use their own creativity to decide how they want to make their presentation. They make scrapbooks and posters, offer tours and demonstrations. It's their choice. They also choose what accomplishments to recognize, highlighting the achievements they most value.

Although self-recognition might seem best suited for white-collar workers who are comfortable making public presentations, at Graniterock everyone gets involved. Ricki Mancebo, a truck driver, discovered a three-way mirror that allows drivers to see better. She checked out the practicality of having one installed on every truck and then oversaw the installation. For Recognition Days, she gave a demonstration of the increased visibility the mirror provided, using her truck as a visual aid.

A branch manager, Carl Jaco, who began nearly twenty years ago as a driver, remembers his first presentation. He, too, had made improvements to his truck. He chose to assemble a book on those improvements, complete with pictures. He gave his presentation, made it through his nervousness, and became excited about self-recognition and Recognition Days. It made such an impact on him that he says he still has the book he created.

There is a lot of energy and excitement around Recognition Days. Even so, some new-hires show a little reluctance to participate. Their managers try to get them to attend at least one Recognition Day before they make their own presentation. Usually that is all it takes to hook them on the idea. People see Recognition Days not only as an opportunity to show off their accomplishments but also as a chance to get to know each other and share ideas while they learn and continue to improve.

So what can we learn from the success of Graniterock Recognition Days?

- Self-recognition isn't a replacement for other types of recognition, but it is a very effective supplement.

- People like having control. Let them decide what accomplishments to recognize and how to present them.
- Some people will be hesitant at first. They may be shy or they may be afraid that others will think they are showing off. Allow them to observe before presenting, and allow presentations that don't require public speaking.
- Success is contagious. As employees observe the accomplishments of their coworkers, they will think of new ways to improve. They will create new challenges and new successes to self-recognize!

The Independent Professional Development Program

Another form of self-recognition in use at Graniterock, although on the surface it may not appear to be recognition at all, is the Individual Professional Development Plan (IPDP). In use since the mid-eighties, the IPDP allows employees to take control of their own growth and development. Individuals work with their managers to describe their major job responsibilities, strengths, and accomplishments. Then they set goals for growth and improvement for the coming year. Finally, they select activities and learning opportunities that will help them achieve those goals. You may be thinking the development plan sounds a little like a performance review, and in a sense it is, but there are some key differences.

The focus is on growth and opportunity. The IPDP really is about professional development. Rather than highlighting the strengths and deficiencies that impact pay increases, it focuses on the learning experiences that will help each person do his or her job better. Managers and employees set developmental objectives and outline activities that will help each person meet those objectives.

Employees choose to participate. The IPDP isn't mandatory. Only employees who see a benefit in the program participate. Employees are the customers in the IPDP process. They only participate if and when they are sold on the idea. In the beginning, a significant number of employees chose not to participate. They had their concerns and reservations. Today, 97 percent of all employees participate. Clearly they see value in the program.

The IPDP is self-directed. Employees set their own objectives and then review them with their managers. Both manager and employee can suggest learning opportunities that will allow the employee to reach his or her objectives. Employees don't always get to take every class or workshop that appeals to them, but if they make a strong case and show how it will positively impact their ability to do their job, they will most likely have the opportunity to take it.

The executive team reviews every IPDP. Once an employee and his or her manager complete the IPDP, the manager reviews it before the other managers and the Executive Committee for feedback. This process ensures that employees are moving in a direction that benefits the company. It also provides every employee with an opportunity for recognition because the executive team learns about each employee's aspirations and accomplishments. It gives employees greater visibility within the organization. In how many organizations do top-level management know the development plans of 97 percent of their employees? The answer is very few. It is a challenge to maintain this level of awareness with nearly eight hundred employees, but Woolpert believes it's worth it. Employees know their improvements will be noticed and that they are important to the organization. Employees know that the executive team cares about their growth and development, and it makes an impression on them.

No copy of the IPDP ever goes into a personnel file. After the executive review, managers meet with the employee to discuss comments and suggestions, and together they develop the final version that will be in effect for the next twelve months. This isn't something that gets filed away. Instead, it becomes a working document, reviewed by the manager and employee regularly throughout the year.

The IPDP recognizes individuals as people worth investing in and capable of determining where they need to grow in order to perform better on the job and advance their careers in the direction they choose. Where Recognition Days focus on the recognition element praise, the IPDP focuses on the elements respect and opportunity. The IPDP meets individual aspirations through education and training while ensuring, through review, that the process is effective for the organization.

Let's review a portion of two hypothetical IPDPs belonging to two entry-level employees—Hakim, a payroll clerk, and George, a new truck driver—to see how their development plans might evolve. Listed below are representative statements that would elicit the same type of responses you would find on the IPDP. We'll use these to show how the IPDP provides a unique form of recognition.

List the major responsibilities that are essential to your job, and put a star by those made possible by last year's development. In this section, employees list their primary responsibilities. Managers can use this section to coach employees on those responsibilities that are most valuable to the company in terms of meeting their objectives. Responsibilities will vary with the job. For our payroll clerk, Hakim, the primary responsibilities might include providing employees with an accurate check and allocating employee time and costs to the appropriate accounts. For our new driver, George, the main responsibilities are operating the vehicle in a safe and courteous manner and ensuring customer satisfaction by delivering the specified product to the right place at the right time. This section of the IPDP also highlights how the job has changed and what new responsibilities have come about because of last year's learning opportunities, recognizing the employee's added value to the company.

Describe what you want to learn during the next twelve months. The employee creates a list of developmental objectives. That list can include increasing product knowledge, improving customer service and safety, and understanding the company objectives, policies, and procedures. Hakim, our payroll clerk, might have objectives that include learning more about the accounting process, so he can improve his ability to allocate time and money appropriately, and getting to know his customers, the employees, so he will better understand their needs. For George, the new driver, one objective might be to learn the streets and terrain of the territory in order to find the quickest and safest routes for his deliveries. A second objective would be to learn how to better serve his customers.

List the corresponding experiences/activities and observable measures that will meet these development objectives. Here we answer the question of how the employee is going to meet his or her objectives. Employees and their managers set short- and long-term goals for training and development. They also list observable measures for new skills learned. Hakim might plan to attend six Recognition Days in order to meet as many of his customers as possible. He might measure success by the number of customers he introduces himself to and learns something about over the next twelve months, or by being able to briefly describe to his manager the job functions of at least three people who work outside of corporate headquarters. To meet his other objective, to learn more about job-costing and allocation, his manager might suggest that he spend some time in the accounting department during the first quarter. George might meet his objectives by spending ten hours studying maps and driving five alternate routes during the first quarter, and demonstrating to the dispatcher, at the end of the second quarter, his ability to identify the quickest and safest route to three job sites. Attending an off-site customer service workshop during the third quarter would meet his objective for learning how to improve customer service.

Notice that most of the IPDP learning opportunities don't involve formal classroom training. Graniterock uses self-study, coaching, and cross-training for many learning opportunities. Management has found that these methods are inexpensive and very effective. They favor cross-training, in particular, because of its ability to improve organizational focus, teamwork, knowledge and skills. That doesn't mean they ignore formal training. All employees attend some Graniterock-sponsored workshops, outside workshops, and classes. Several Graniterock People are very proud to have learned to read as a result of the training they received. Learning opportunities come in all shapes and forms.

A longtime employee told me, "When the IPDP was first implemented, people couldn't always see the relevance. After all, why does a driver need to be trained in customer service? Our focus was too narrow. Now that focus has broadened, and most of us see the value of the IPDP in our growth and development within the company."

So what can we learn from the development plan process at Graniterock?

- Make as many senior-level managers as possible aware of the development plans of each employee. This visibility improves employee career options. When employees see multiple opportunities for growth within their organizations they are more likely to stay with the organization and stay enthusiastic.
- Don't treat the development plan as a performance review and don't make it a requirement. Employees should see the development plan as an opportunity to learn and grow. Use it to recognize their value to the organization.
- Be creative in selecting learning opportunities. Don't limit your options to formal training. Consider mentoring, self-directed learning, and cross-training. Learning opportunities are everywhere.
- Work with employees to create and implement the plan. Give them as much control as possible while helping them to improve their value to the company.

Missed Opportunity

Recognition Days and the IPDP are at the core of Graniterock recognition. They rely upon individuals to know what they need and then to provide it for themselves. This kind of autonomy has a powerful effect on employee satisfaction and has helped to give Graniterock a reputation as a thriving employee-friendly company focused on quality products and services.

Self-recognition is a powerful and underutilized form of recognition. Few organizations or managers ask employees to recognize themselves. They are missing an excellent opportunity. By adding self-recognition into your existing recognition mix, you can encourage employees to showcase their most important accomplishments. When employees control their own recognition, they receive validation for what is most meaningful to them. After all, who knows what an individual wants more than that individual? Self-recognition allows management a glimpse into what employees value so they can use that information to create other forms of recognition that will be meaningful. And finally, self-recognition adds to the frequency of recognition. It increases the possibility that every employee will feel sufficiently recognized.

TAKING ACTION

Everyone Can

- Acknowledge their own success. Most of us are in the habit of ignoring the good that we do and focusing on our mistakes. Keep a journal of your accomplishments. Refer back to it when you need a boost. Use it to keep your résumé up to date.
- Tell others about his or her accomplishments. There is nothing wrong with announcing in your team meeting, "I'm happy to report I have finished my certification training," or telling a

coworker, "Wow, that was a difficult customer, but I finally solved her problem." Take the occasional opportunity to talk about your successes.

- Encourage others to tell you what they accomplish. If you know they have done something well, ask them about it. You will help make self-recognition a part of how your team operates.

Managers

- Encourage employees in your department to acknowledge their own accomplishments. Make self-recognition acceptable. Spend a few minutes in your weekly meeting asking employees to recount a success from the previous week.
- Plan for success. Work with employees to set development goals. Encourage them to explore a variety of learning opportunities. Review and celebrate their progress and help them recognize their own potential.
- Convince employees that they have an obligation to share their successes because everyone benefits when they do. The answer to how one person overcame a particular challenge might provide the answer to someone else's pressing issue. Like they discovered at Pella Windows & Doors, innovation breeds innovation.
- Make self-recognition fun. Celebrate. Get employees excited about participating. The quality of recognition will go up, and you will have an excellent learning experience for everyone involved.

PART **3**

Making
Recognition Work

chapter 9

A Lesson from a Fortune Cookie

Make Recognition Specific and Relevant

Crack open a fortune cookie and you get a fortune that's nearly always true. Yet you will rarely find the message interesting. Why? Because it is vague. In the writer's attempt to make the fortune relevant to everyone, it becomes relevant to no one.

You can learn a recognition lesson from the fortune cookie.

Vague recognition that could apply to anyone doesn't leave people feeling recognized. The Employee of the Month Award is the classic example. Typically, there are no set criteria for receiving the award. It's simply given to an employee identified as doing a good

job. Without set criteria, Employee of the Month leaves workers asking questions: "How is this month's winner a better employee than I
am?" "Am I doing a good job?" "What exactly do you have to do
to become employee of the month?" If employees can't find satisfac-
tory answers to these questions, the title quickly becomes meaningless. People won't strive to win the award if they don't know what it
takes to win it. If, by chance, they do win, their sense of pride will be
limited because they won't know what the award represents.

When you play a game, you want to know the rules before you begin.

Think of the last time you played a game: a sport, board game,
computer or video game, anything that you like to play for fun.
Did you know the rules of the game before you began? Did everyone play by the rules? What would happen if you all played by different rules or someone cheated? Your first reaction might be
frustration. You might attempt to get everyone to play fairly by the
same rules, but if that failed, you would probably lose interest and
quit. The same thing is true with recognition. When recognition is
ineffective, frequently it is because no one knows the rules of the
recognition "game."

Playing by the rules means you judge and recognize performance based on preestablished criteria. It builds trust when you play
by the rules, and employees who work in an atmosphere of trust
are happier and more willing to work cooperatively. So how do
you establish the rules of recognition? You begin by identifying the
values, goals, and behaviors that lead to success.

What Do Values Have to Do with Recognition?

Microsoft Great Plains Business Solutions has a mission and shared
values that are integral to their culture. They believe recognition

based on what they value reinforces their organizational culture because it allows employees the opportunity to see examples of what is outstanding. They offer many different awards, each emphasizing different organizational values.

Their Heritage Award[1] recognizes excellence in customer service and is presented to two or three outstanding employees each year. Coworkers nominate potential recipients, describing in detail how the nominee embodies the values represented by the award. The guidelines for nomination are laid out clearly, as you can see in this excerpt from their nomination form:

Microsoft Great Plains Business Solutions' Mission:
    To improve the lives and business of Partners and Customers.

    Shared Values, we must:
• Foster a close relationship with our Partners and Customers that will result in a better understanding of what they are experiencing.
• Encourage innovation, independent action, team spirit, and personal growth in all Team Members.
• Ensure that everything we do reflects exceptional levels of quality.
• Demonstrate integrity in all business relationships.

The Heritage Award (Excellence in Customer Service):

Having a common history is not enough to unify a company. You need a shared heritage. History only tells where you've been and what you've done; heritage reveals who you are and what you're about. As human beings, we need to identify with more than a product or a paycheck. We need a context of values and ideals that give meaning to what we do every day. That's heritage. And from the beginning, our heritage has been customer service.

This award honors an individual who has shown resourcefulness, determination, and personal integrity, overcoming obstacle after obstacle to do what's right by the customer. Not only have they enriched our heritage of customer service, but in so doing have proven it to be life affirming as well as profitable.

Ask a Microsoft Great Plains Business Solutions employee why his coworker won the Heritage Award, and he will know. When the award is presented and the nomination read, everyone learns why the nominee was chosen to receive the award. They know the nominee's actions embody the values that they all share. Ask a recipient if the award has meaning, and you will get a resounding "yes."

Values Help Avoid Unintended Results

Recognition that isn't based on strongly held organizational values gets limited results, no results, or the wrong results. Setting goals, particularly goals accompanied by financial incentives, without creating a strong foundation in values is potentially dangerous. Consider the following example:

> For a chemical manufacturer, a top concern should be safety. Their people should live and breathe safety. If everything they do isn't focused around promoting safety, then a goal to reduce the number of accidents reported would only lead to a reduction in the number of accidents *reported*, not necessarily a reduction in the number of accidents occurring. This is especially true if recognition is accompanied by a financial incentive.

Even if the manufacturer puts a high value on safety, some employees would still find it tempting to not report minor accidents if it meant they would get a bonus. To reduce the possibility of this happening, management needs to confirm that they recognize and reward only desired behaviors. They need to ask themselves the following questions:

- Do we emphasize the importance of *being* safe rather than *appearing* safe?
- Do we value consistency in following safety protocol rather than having speed and profit our primary concerns?
- Do we recognize and reward ideas that will improve safety rather than proving everything is perfect the way it is?
- Do we recognize and reward people for reporting and correcting violations rather than overlooking and concealing violations?

Management's goals and actions have to clearly support the company's key values. In the chemical manufacturer's case, the key value is safety. That value should be built into everything they do, from business strategies to the recognition they offer. There should be no doubt about their intentions.

Remember, you are defining the rules of the game. Clarifying values helps to define the objective. It begins to answer the questions, "What do we have to do to win?" and "How do we know when we have won?" The answers to these questions determine how employees will behave.

Values Provide Purpose and Meaning

Have you ever heard an employee say, "What's the point?" They may be burned out and in need of serious guidance or coaching to get them back on track. Or it may simply be that they don't understand how their work fits into the bigger picture. An understanding of their value to the team and/or organization motivates most people.

Can the people who work with you describe what your organization, division, or department values? Do they understand your business model, your mission statement? If not, you need to communicate that information.

Disney's core values are imagination and wholesomeness. This is such an important part of Disney that not only do employees know their values, so do their customers. Disney does an excellent job communicating its values. Hewlett-Packard did such a good job communicating its values that they were able to maintain those values over the long term. Since their humble beginnings in a garage, Hewlett-Packard has stated that it values the individual, quality, reliability, and the community. More than a half-century later, management was still talking about those values. They referred to them as the "Rules of the Garage." By that time, some were questioning whether HP still lived the same values. Assuming they were, the "rules" were a clever way of packaging their values in the roots of the organization.

Dell Computer has a strong business model that stresses the value of communication. This is demonstrated in its commitment to keeping only five days of inventory on hand.[2] If a supplier is slow delivering a component, Purchasing must communicate that information to Sales. Sales then drives demand by promoting alternative components to their customers. If, on the other hand, demand for a product drops for forty-eight hours, Sales needs to tell Purchasing so they can reduce their reorder level. Employees understand the strategy. Dell has communicated the importance of low inventory levels, and employees do their part to ensure success.

Know what you value. Know where your organization is going, and know how you plan to get there. Communicate your strategy clearly and frequently. Provide employees with the necessary resources. Work these things into the fiber of your organization or department. Then use recognition to reinforce what is important.

Recognition tied to commonly held values and goals can be extremely meaningful. I learned this lesson firsthand while consulting for Raytek Corporation, an international company that manufactures infrared thermometers. Years ago, when they first became my client, I was touring their offices and noticed something intriguing. Everywhere I looked, people's cubicles had plastic apples on display. When I asked about them, I learned that the apple awards were given, along with an extra vacation day, to employees who used no sick time during the previous year. As my guide continued to explain, I learned that the company placed a high value on saving money. Much of their corporate culture was based around that value. The people at Raytek were proud of their ability to improve profitability by reducing costs, and management acknowledged their efforts. One way employees helped to save money was by using sick time only when they were sick, rather than using the time as discretionary personal days. The days off were a valued reward, but the apples were a lasting symbol of their contribution. Employees were proud of what the apples represented.

Tie Recognition to Performance

Peak performers want to do work that matters. For their 1999 book *First, Break All the Rules*,[3] Marcus Buckingham and Curt Coffman of the Gallup Organization sifted through more than a million interviews to determine what matters most to top performers. They found twelve workplace characteristics most critical to these employees. According to the research, one of those characteristics concerns whether the "mission/purpose of my company makes me feel my job is important."

Employees are more willing to take initiative when they understand the mission, values, strategic plan, and goals of the organization. Being able to see how these relate to individual performance is motivating. Part of your job, in recognizing individuals, is to establish a clear link between the organization's values and goals and the individual's goals and behaviors. The link between these two is shared goals.

Shared Goals and Performance

Effective organizations set high-level performance goals. Each level in an organization then sets goals that align with all the entities they report to. The goals of a business unit may only need to align with those of the organization, while the goals of a cross-functional team might need to align with the goals of the organization, their division, and each of their individual departments.

To illustrate this point, take a look at how the various departments of a large nonprofit agency might align themselves with a company-wide goal to reduce costs.

- Client Services looks for more cost-effective ways to serve their clients.
- Volunteer Education chooses to implement an on-line learning solution to reduce the expense associated with traveling around the country to provide training.
- The Publications department tests the response rates of a direct mail campaign using postcards instead of letters. They know that if response rates are comparable, it will mean a significant savings on postage.

At each level, groups pursue separate goals, but their goals all align with the cost-cutting goal of the organization.

> *Four-step collaborative process for setting shared goals:*
>
> (1) Review the values, mission, vision, strategies, and goals you share with other parts of your organization.
> (2) Brainstorm possible shared goals for your group.
> (3) Identify and prioritize shared goals.
> (4) Get buy-in from group members.

So how are shared goals developed? They can be developed by management and dictated to employees, but you will find it more effective to use a collaborative process. Let employees help set shared goals, and they will have a better understanding and greater ownership of those goals. They will also be more likely to achieve them.

Setting collaborative goals together provides the group with a strong sense of clarity about what those goals mean. This improves employees' sense of purpose. To further emphasize that sense of purpose, recognize groups when they achieve a shared goal. You might celebrate the achievement of small goals with an announcement and donuts or pizza (employees and managers alike say that food is a requirement for any celebration!). For bigger goals, dinner for the group, along with a formal acknowledgment, might be appropriate. Regardless of the form it takes, when you recognize shared successes, you provide an opportunity for everyone in the group to be a winner.

Individual Goals and Performance

Group goals provide a framework for individual performance goals. Understanding what motivates the organization, division, department, or team helps employees align their own goals and gives them a greater sense of purpose.

The Volunteer Education department of our previously mentioned nonprofit shares the organization-wide goal to reduce costs. They know that on-line training can be very cost-effective in some instances, so they choose, as their department goal, to implement an on-line learning solution to help educate the agency's volunteers.

Several members of the department set individual goals to become familiar with available learning technologies. Together they will select the most cost-effective solution. Other members choose to focus on which courses can best adapt to the on-line format and provide the most cost savings. Alex embraces his department's goal to implement on-line learning but chooses to balance the department's cost-saving efforts with his own efforts around another shared value—customer service. Volunteers are the customers of their department, so with his manager's guidance, Alex chooses to survey volunteers to determine what they want from training. Alex is excited about the project because he is clear that his contribution will make their on-line learning solution better.

When the survey is complete, Alex has successfully captured the volunteer perspective; he knows what they want. Alex's manager asks him to act as the implementation team expert on that perspective. While Alex is the obvious choice for this role, the new responsibility is also a form of recognition. It recognizes the value of Alex's contribution to the team.

Help employees select goals that align with your shared values and goals. Clarify tasks and roles so that each person can recognize his or her own unique contribution. Help employees discover, understand, and even extend the magnitude of their contribution, and you help them to recognize the value of their own achievements. In turn, they will be more enthusiastic and productive.

Recognize individuals who achieve their goals using the approaches discussed earlier in this book. With smaller goals you will probably want to do this one-to-one. A private verbal acknowledgment or a hand-written or e-mailed note is appropriate. If the goal was a significant milestone, announce it in a team meeting or provide a gift certificate when you acknowledge the achievement, whatever is most appropriate for the individual.

If you need more help in setting goals, refer to Douglas K. Smith's book, *Make Success Measurable!*[4]

High-Performance Behaviors

Employees like recognition that is specific, relevant, and *frequent*. According to the Gallup survey (*First, Break All the Rules*) mentioned earlier in this chapter, peak performers want to be recognized at least every seven days. This presents a challenge. If a manager helps each employee set and achieve about ten goals for the year and recognizes the employee for every achievement, recognition is still too infrequent.

Few managers could handle the workload that would accompany setting fifty-two goals per employee per year. There are two solutions for the frequency problem that are more manageable and effective. The first solution is to get everyone involved in the process of recognition: team leaders, coworkers, even the individual himself. Look back to part two of this book for ideas on how to do this. Second, and the point I want to address here, is that you want to recognize behaviors as well goals. Together these two things will expand the opportunities for recognition exponentially without overburdening you, the manager.

> PROBLEM: Many goals take months, even years to accomplish and recognition needs to be frequent to be effective.
>
> SOLUTION: Recognize both *accomplishments* and the *behaviors* that lead to those accomplishments.

Recognized behaviors, like goals, need to be specific. When someone tells you they appreciate that you offer several possible solutions when you present a problem, you know exactly what they value. You can't say the same thing when they compliment you on your positive attitude. Do they mean they like that you don't mention potential problems? Do they like that you tell jokes in the break room every morning? Or do they mean that it's great that you let them push you around without complaint? With vague recognition, it's left up to the imagination.

> VAGUE: Positive attitude
>
> SPECIFIC: Treats customers and coworkers with respect.
>   Tackles projects outside the scope of her job responsibilities.
>   Rarely complains, prefers to look for solutions.
>   Brings a bit of fun or humor to every meeting.
>   Treats failure as a learning opportunity.

Clear, specific recognition of behaviors is meaningful, regardless of whether it comes from the manager or a coworker. It provides guidance, strengthening the working relationship with the person giving the recognition. Compare the impact of these two thank-you notes:

> Jan,
>   Thank you for your work on the new accounts receivable system. Your efforts are appreciated.
>   Thank you, Sara

While many employees would be thrilled to receive this much recognition from a manager or coworker, consider how much more meaningful the next version is:

> Jan,
>   Just a quick note to let you know how much I appreciate the initiative you've taken with our new accounts receivable system. I understand some of the processes are less than intuitive and that many members of the implementation team are already frustrated. Your efforts to understand the quirks of the system and assist your team members in overcoming them will help us to achieve our goal of a flawless transition and help us to serve our customers better when the new system is in place.
>   Thank you, Sara

It takes more time and effort to be specific, and people appreciate that effort. Send a thank-you note like the one in the second example, and you tell the recipient she is important because you know precisely what she did that was commendable, and you took the time to tell her. Send a thank-you note like the second example, and you offer recognition that positively impacts performance.

Specific Recognition Has Lasting Impact

A mother of a young Staples office supply employee told me, "[At Staples] they have 'I noticed' cards. There is no value attached. It's just a note from the manager saying what she noticed the employee doing. My son has every one he's received posted on a board at home!"

Specific recognition tells employees exactly what they are doing that is valued. On each of the Staples' employee's "I noticed" cards, his manager had communicated what behavior she considered commendable and told the employee that he exhibited that behavior. This young employee responded to being "noticed."

Remember the fortune cookie. Vague, unspecific recognition that could apply to anyone leaves employees feeling unrecognized. Specific, detailed recognition, based on your organizational goals and values, is most meaningful. Communicate "the rules," the specific goals, desired behaviors, and intended purpose of recognition. Use recognition to emphasize the group and individual efforts and results. Work to provide fair, specific, and frequent recognition, and you'll provide recognition with meaning.

TAKING ACTION

- Evaluate your recognition efforts by asking yourself these questions:
    - Is my recognition focused on the most important issues?
    - Have I clarified how recognized behaviors and outcomes support what I value?
    - Am I confident I'm recognizing the intended behaviors and outcomes and not others?
    - Have I achieved the results I anticipated?
- Offer specific, meaningful recognition by telling employees exactly what they did and why you value their behavior or contribution.

Measure for Results

Why Measure?

Sports teams keep score. They also track averages, handicaps, assists, and receptions. Anything that measures performance gets reported. Statistics give players objective feedback. When a player receives the award for most valuable player, good statistics usually back it up. Those statistics help to make the award fair and consistent from year to year. Measurement makes the award relevant to both players and spectators. In your organization, you measure for the same reasons—to track performance. When you measure and then use that information in your recognition, you provide objective feedback and make the award relevant to recipients and observers alike.

A Toastmasters, International club in Amherst, New York,[1] provides a good example of measurement in action. Clubs and associations have always had difficulty getting members to take on leadership roles. Lacking the ability to offer financial rewards, volunteer organizations have to rely on other ways to motivate members. This Toastmasters club in Amherst previously had a great deal of difficulty getting people to volunteer long enough to gain the experience needed to take on the role of president. Members would serve as Treasurer or VP of Education and then step down. Few members felt ready or willing to take on the responsibilities of president.

The club needed to find a way to get members to rotate through all the officer positions, gain experience, and then step into the president's role as the culminating activity. The question that faced the group was "How do we get members to step up to the challenge?" They found an answer. They started measuring and recognizing participation and got results!

WHAT THEY VALUE: Volunteers for leadership positions.

THEIR GOAL: To have members hold every leadership position.

WHAT THEY MEASURE: Which leadership positions members have held.

THE RECOGNITION: The title of Terrific Toastmaster.

After a member has served six months in every leadership role, their name is engraved on a plaque and their contribution highlighted in the club newsletter.

It sounds simple and it is, but the results are still impressive. Members who had previously been reluctant now challenge themselves to become Terrific Toastmasters, and the pool of potential presidents has increased significantly.

What to Measure?

Look at your organizational values, business strategies, and goals before you decide what to measure. They can provide focus. Measures should provide tangible proof that your organization is achieving its goals within the boundaries of its values.

As mentioned in the previous chapter, you can usually achieve your goals by more than one method. With a strong incentive, people will achieve success in ways you never considered. As you'll see in the following example, some of their methods can produce undesired results:

> To reduce costs, one strategy used by some HMOs is to measure the number of referrals doctors make to specialists and base bonuses on that measurement. The fewer referrals doctors make, the bigger their bonus. If the HMO holds two key values: profits and the health and well-being of their patients, their objective might be to limit only unnecessary referrals. The problem is the only value they are measuring and rewarding for—is profit.
>
> Most doctors will choose to continue to stress patient health on their own, but some will get caught up in the measures and rewards. These doctors will produce fewer referrals, reasonable or not, increasing HMO profitability and their own bonuses. But at the same time, they will jeopardize patient health.

While this is less likely to happen with recognition than it is with an incentive such as a bonus, it is still true that you are more likely to achieve what you reinforce. To achieve the HMO's goal of reducing unnecessary referrals, it will need to find a way to also measure a doctor's commitment to patient health and well-being.

Carefully tie measures to your existing values and goals. Verify that what you are measuring only measures the desired result.

Look for relationships between your organization's values, goals, and measures. The following example will help you make stronger connections between values, goals, measures, and recognition. In this example, the goal is to reduce annual turnover, the percentage of the work force that leaves each year. If the current turnover rate is 32 percent a year, and the organization wants to reduce that by one-third to 22 percent, reducing turnover to 22 percent a year becomes the measurable goal.

VALUES	MEASURE	MEASURABLE GOAL
high job satisfaction	employee turnover	reduce turnover
productivity		from 32% to 22% annually
profitability		

Note the relationship that exists between the three values and the corresponding measurable goal. High job satisfaction results in reduced turnover, and reduced turnover typically results in increased productivity and profitability. If this organization focuses on reducing turnover by increasing job satisfaction, it should see improvement in productivity and profitability as well. The following two examples show how recognition might support these values and goals:

- A manager challenges employees in his department to help reduce turnover. He emphasizes the impact that everyone has in creating a positive work environment. Employees create departmental values and related goals to help them achieve their turnover goal. When they succeed in reducing turnover by one-third, the manager plans a celebration to announce their success.
- A VP asks a manager who already has achieved less than 22 percent annual turnover while maintaining a high job satisfaction rate to mentor another manager in their division. This

recognizes the successful manager while providing information for the other manager on what is already working.

Neither of these opportunities for recognition is likely to have
unanticipated results. Both offer values-based recognition. But if
the executive team instead decides to offer managers bonuses
based on their departments' turnover rate, it can blur the connection between results and values. A manager might keep unpro-
ductive employees or refuse to promote to other departments in
order to keep his or her turnover rate down and receive the bonus.
Recognition accompanied by financial rewards requires a system
of checks and balances. The executive team would need to consider which methods of reducing turnover would be undesirable
and adjust for that. A balanced scorecard approach using multiple
variables such as employee job satisfaction, productivity, and profitability as well as turnover rates would be one way to reinforce
all three values and their goal of reduced turnover.

Taking Stock of Current Measures

Assess your current methods of measurement. Note what you
measure and how your measures relate to your values and goals.
Use this information to clarify your recognition objectives and generate recognition ideas based on measurable criteria.

Consider getting help in selecting appropriate measures. Admin-
istrative groups within your organization can be terrific resources.
They may already track much of the information you need and can
help you to define new measures. Finance already tracks profits, revenue, and costs. Human Resources probably tracks sick days taken,
turnover and employee satisfaction rates, safety records, and the percent of employees mentored or trained. Lots of information should
be readily available throughout the organization. Consider statistics
such as productivity, defect rates, follow-through on qualified leads,
rate of repeat business, number and nature of complaints, and customer satisfaction ratings.

What Others Are Measuring

System up-time at customer sites—Sun Microsystems

"The most important commitment we can make is to share our customers' risk." —Scott McNealy, CEO

Employee satisfaction—Gymboree Corp.

"If people aren't happy working here, that's going to show in our products and services." —Gary White, CEO

Attendance—Women's NBA

"Attendance generates revenue, but it also generates team morale and sales momentum." —Val Ackerman, President

Company culture—PowerBar Inc.

"We measure 41 statements about our company culture. . . . Two things are going to help us compete successfully: our brand and our people. And because our brand is managed by our people, people are what matter most. For us, that means tracking company culture." —Brian Maxwell, Cofounder & CEO

Measure What Matters
Fast Company, May 1999

Data Collection

In this section you will learn to select data sources and make appropriate use of the information you gather. When considering the validity of any information you use, hold it up to the following criteria:

- *Measurements should* provide quantifiable data.
- *Measurements should* be consistent over time.
- *Measurements should* create an accurate picture of current conditions.

Make sure you can quantify the information you gather. For example, how do you measure for job satisfaction? Is it enough to observe that employees seem happier? No, it isn't. Measuring takes a vague concept and makes it tangible. You can find numbers that relate to job satisfaction. As already mentioned, turnover rate is one good indicator. Number of sick days taken can be another. You can find many more. Whichever indicators you choose, make sure they are measurable.

Be consistent over time. Use the same measurement for an extended period. This will help you to identify trends in your data.

Use measurement to create an accurate picture of current conditions. The big question to ask yourself is "Am I really measuring what I think I am measuring?" If additional training can improve job satisfaction, does that mean the number of training days taken is a good indicator of job satisfaction? It might be, but if people are required to complete training they think is worthless, job satisfaction may actually go down. To avoid misinterpreting data and making erroneous assumptions, use multiple measures from a variety of sources. For instance, number of days trained, current turnover rate, and the results of a job satisfaction survey would provide a more balanced picture.

Quantitative Resources for Measuring Success

Review of financial and operational documents

As mentioned earlier, your organization already tracks data. Balance sheets, income statements, financial ratios, and production, service, and regulatory reports all provide excellent quantifiable (measurable) information. Most of this information has already been compiled, using the same methodology, for long periods of time. It's a free source of data that should help you to identify trends. See what's already available before you choose new methods of data collection.

Questionnaires and surveys

Questionnaires and surveys are great for gathering opinions. They can provide inexpensive, consistent, and quantifiable data that offer a candid, accurate picture—but only if people believe you will keep their responses confidential and only if you can elicit enough responses to make your survey representative. Use caution when creating your own survey or questionnaire; poorly designed questions can influence participant responses and skew the results. Unless you are experienced in survey design, you may be better off purchasing predesigned surveys or having an expert create one for you. For more information *see* chapter 12 and the section on job satisfaction surveys.

When you choose to do a questionnaire or survey, keep in mind that the people you survey will have an expectation of change. Tell respondents why you are gathering information and what changes they can expect as a result of the survey. If you ask your customers what new features they would like to see in your product and then fail to deliver an updated version, you will see customer satisfaction drop. The same is true with employees.

Qualitative Resources for Deeper Analysis

One-on-one interviews

One-on-one interviews can provide both quantitative and qualitative information. Using them to gather quantitative data, however, isn't the most practical use because they are more time-intensive and therefore more expensive to administer than a survey or questionnaire.

One-on-one interviews are best used to dig deeper into survey results. One-on-one interviews can help you discover *why* respondents answered the way they did. This additional information, while not measurable, is valuable because it helps to clarify survey results, allowing you to learn more about the issues the survey reveals.

There are a couple of potential problems to consider when using one-on-one interviews. One, because of the lack of anonymity, you will get less candid responses if interviewees are uncomfortable with the interviewer. Two, interviewers with a bias toward a specific outcome can skew results by leading respondents toward their preferred response.

Focus groups

With a focus group a skilled facilitator provides the topic and guides the group through a discussion. Some of the advantages and disadvantages are similar to those found in one-on-one interviews. Like one-on-one interviews, focus groups provide an excellent opportunity to explore unanticipated issues and clarify survey results. They are also better for gathering qualitative rather than quantitative information. And like the negative impact an interviewer can have in a one-on-one interview, a focus group can be adversely affected by choosing the wrong facilitator.

Focus groups also have their own unique advantages and disadvantages. Being part of a group can stimulate participants to talk about issues that they might not have considered in a one-on-one interview. At the same time, if participants of the focus group know each other, they may not be willing to openly discuss the topic being explored.

Observation

Observation isn't appropriate as a measurement tool, but it is valuable for recognizing behaviors. Providing recognition that works requires managers to gather data by observation and then use that information to correct or recognize the behaviors that affect performance. They might observe whether employees are friendly to customers, keep the production area clean, or offer suggestions for improvement. Observation is also the basis of most employee-nominated awards. It is appropriate for this purpose so long as the awards recognize clearly articulated behaviors.

Choose your data sources carefully. Determine what is appropriate in each situation. Have multiple measures and use those measures in your recognition efforts. Remember, measurement helps make recognition more meaningful. Just as sports fans appreciate statistics on their favorite teams and players, employees like "knowing the score." Measure workplace performance, and you provide an objective yardstick that will help you create meaningful and memorable recognition.

TAKING ACTION

- Provide recognition based on the data you collect.
- Measure your ability to meet your goals using quantifiable, time-tested data.
- Collect information from a variety of sources.
- Look to existing resources for measurement data before developing new data sources.
- Use qualitative data to support quantitative data.
- Ground your measures in values to help counter the success-by-any-means mind-set.

One Size
Doesn't Fit All

Personalized Individual Recognition

Picture the following scenario. Alli is responsible for producing the specifications for her team's latest project. Maritza, another member of her team, volunteers to stay late
one evening to help Alli finish those specifications. Maritza
didn't have to do that, so to show her appreciation, Alli
gives her a Mars™ candy bar. She tells her it's for "out of
this world" teamwork. Alli gives a candy bar to everyone
whose assistance she considers noteworthy. It's a clever idea
that emphasizes Alli's point—that Maritza's contribution
was exceptional. It's a gesture that Alli hopes will
strengthen their working relationship. The problem is,
Maritza is a diabetic. Alli's choice of a recognition symbol,

a candy bar, shows Maritza that while her contributions matter, her personal needs don't. Instead of strengthening their relationship, it may damage it.

Employees subjected to mass recognition, with no appreciation of their unique needs and interests, feel only half-acknowledged. To be most effective, you need to acknowledge both the achievement and the person behind the achievement. This is true of all recognition, but it's especially important with individual recognition. You can't always consider everyone's unique concerns when you offer group recognition, but there is no excuse for impersonal individual recognition.

Some people will argue that individual recognition is counterproductive. They say it creates jealousy and resentment, and that the only way to promote teamwork is to recognize the entire team. Team recognition is important. So is organization-wide and departmental recognition. They can create a sense of cohesiveness. But the importance of group recognition doesn't preclude the need for individual recognition. People still want to know they're valued as individuals, particularly those employees who are most engaged and productive—the peak performers. Even if they consider themselves team players (and most do), high-achieving employees don't want all of the credit to go to the team.

An employee from IBM said his manager sends a handwritten note to each direct report on the anniversary of his or her hire date. The note recounts the employee's contributions for the year, describing how he or she is important to the department. People in his department look forward to receiving and sharing these notes with each other. The manager recognizes the unique contributions of his people. In return they feel a sense of loyalty to him.

Recognition is most meaningful when it takes into account the talents, skills, concerns, needs, affiliations, and accomplishments of the people you are recognizing. People want you to know something about them before you choose how to recognize them. They are especially impressed if the recognition is unique and especially selected for them.

> A maintenance officer in the air force received an award that he considered both unique and meaningful. The award was a hand-drawn picture of the three types of aircraft he maintained, mounted with photos of the eighteen people who worked with him in his section. He said this one-of-a-kind award was the most memorable recognition he had ever received.

The Process for Individualizing Recognition

When you take time to listen and get to know an individual, what they value, and the quality of their work, you are offering a powerful form of recognition. Regardless of whether you are the person's supervisor, someone from another department, the CEO, or a person they work with every day, personal attention gives recognition greater impact.

To better focus your attention and increase the positive impact, consider using this three-step process for individualizing recognition:

(1) Identify how each individual contributes.
(2) Determine personal recognition preferences.
(3) Recognize unique contributions with personalized recognition.

In the following sections, you will learn how to best accomplish each step.

Identify How the Individual Contributes

*"Assess productivity by asking workers
what tasks they do, what they believe they should be
contributing to the company, and what hampers them
in getting the work done."* —PETER DRUCKER[1]

If your work is affected by the contribution of someone else, you should be offering individualized recognition of specific accomplishments and behaviors. Regardless of your role in the organization, pay attention to how others contribute to your ability to accomplish your goals. Use that information to acknowledge how they have helped you. Step one—identify how each individual contributes—helps you to provide simple recognition that works.

The Manager's or Supervisor's Responsibility

If you're a manager or supervisor, there is a lot more you can do. Traditionally, it's your responsibility to help employees identify how they, as individuals, will contribute to the organization and then track their progress. Do it right and the process itself is loaded with inherent recognition. Employees want to know they are making a contribution. They also want to know someone with the ability to influence the direction of their career is interested in their progress and wants to help them advance. When you show employees that you want them to succeed, they know they are valued. They feel recognized.

The Contribution Conversation

The easiest way to find out how employees can better contribute to the organization (and therefore improve their level of recognition) is to ask them. As the manager, you should schedule at least one meeting per year with each employee to discuss how their job contributes to the values and goals of the organization. The purpose of this meeting isn't to assess performance, although that's certainly a related conversation. The purpose of this meeting is to develop a better understanding of how the employee views his or her job and to correct any misconceptions about the importance of his or her contribution.

To begin this conversation, explain the purpose of the interview and review the organization's values and goals. The following example shows how this discussion might progress:

> "Ray, I asked you here this afternoon to discuss how your role as salesperson helps us to achieve our organization's goals and maintain our values. Just so we are clear, I am not questioning whether your contribution has value. I simply want to ensure you are doing work that you see as valuable.
>
> As you know, XYZ Corporation has based its business model on four key values: profit, innovation, quality, and adaptability. The goals for the coming year are to release one new product, upgrade three products based on customer preference surveys, and find a new market for two existing products."

This statement sets the stage for the questions that follow:

How do you see your work contributing? This question, or something similar, helps the employee explore his job responsibilities and relate those responsibilities back to the values and goals of the organization. Again, make sure the employee understands that you are not questioning the value of his work, but want to discover how he *perceives* the value of his contribution.

> Ray responds that, as a salesperson, his sales contribute to the profitability of the company. Also, the company uses

the information he gathers from customers to discover consumer preferences. This information helps the company to develop new products that will be in high demand.

What tasks are you currently assigned that don't support these organizational values and goals? The purpose of this question is two-part. It helps to streamline operations by uncovering redundant, unnecessary responsibilities, and it helps employees understand how their specific tasks contribute to the values and goals of the organization.

Ray thinks the time he spends compiling statistics on the number of lost sales is a waste of time, which may or may not be true. It's worth exploring and clarifying.

Can these tasks be modified to make them more relevant? This question explores, in greater depth, the employee's response to the preceding question. You can encourage the employee to make appropriate changes to how he performs a task so he can contribute in a more meaningful way.

Ray's manager suggests that, along with the number of lost sales, Ray could track why the prospect didn't purchase their product. This information could be used to develop, upgrade, and expand their current markets.

What new responsibilities would allow you to contribute to an even greater extent? This question explores how an employee would make his or her contribution more relevant and valuable and helps the manager provide opportunities for growth.

Ray tells his manager he wants to work with Research and Development, facilitating a series of customer focus groups that explore customer preference in depth.

In this conversation, you see Ray and his manager clarify Ray's value to the organization. It provides Ray with the opportunity to recognize his own contribution, while the manager learns how Ray perceives that contribution. Ray learns something about how his responsibilities actually impact the organization. His manager helps him modify some of the tasks that he sees as a waste of time and shows him the value of others. Together they also explore new opportunities, discuss their feasibility, and set appropriate action items that will make Ray's work more meaningful. The discussion and resulting changes show Ray that his manager is aware of his value to the organization and supports his desire to have an even more positive impact.

This discussion can provide you and your employees with important information. You learn what they value and how they perceive the jobs they do. This information allows you to stay up to date on how employees already contribute and how they want to contribute in the future. Employees learn how their responsibilities affect their organization, and this helps them make a more meaningful contribution. Because you, as the manager, are aware of their value, your employees feel recognized for both their contribution and their potential contribution.

Determine Personal Recognition Preferences

Employees across the country had diverse answers when asked about recognition that had lasting impact: As mentioned earlier, one said that being asked to take the president's place on a panel discussion was an honor she would never forget. Another valued his manager's willingness to have him work whenever and wherever he wanted, as long as the work was done. A third said having her direct supervisor praise her work to the department head was something she appreciated.

Ask ten people what type of recognition they most value and you will most likely get ten different answers. Preferences vary with each individual. To see firsthand how different recognition preferences can be, copy the survey on the next page, complete it yourself, and then ask friends and family members to do the same. You will see that your preferences and those of the people you survey vary significantly.

In my interviews, few people specifically said it was the personalization of the recognition they received that made it memorable. Even so, as they described memorable recognition, a pattern became clear; personalized recognition has more meaning. This makes sense when you consider that personalized recognition makes a positive statement about the quality of the relationship between giver and receiver.

One employee of a high-tech company was definite about what makes recognition high-impact for her. She told me her most memorable award was an overnight trip for her and her husband to a woodland resort area where they would be able to hike and spend time outdoors. It was memorable because, according to this employee, "it was tailored specifically to what I like to do." The fact that her supervisor knew her well enough to select that trip as a form of recognition was invaluable. The personalized recognition she received strengthened her relationship with, and sense of loyalty to, that supervisor.

Information about hobbies, job aspirations, friends, family, and even whether someone is gregarious or shy will help you to discover what each person would appreciate. Regardless of your role in the organization, you show people that they are important to you, the team, and the organization when you select recognition based on their individual interests.

Remember: Just knowing an individual's aspirations
and interests is a form of recognition.

Which Do You Prefer?

CHECK ALL THAT APPLY

- ❏ Time off in exchange for the extra hours worked to meet a project deadline.

- ❏ A gift certificate for dinner for two as acknowledgment for a glowing letter of praise from a client.

- ❏ A catered lunch for your department to celebrate an achievement.

- ❏ The ability to determine your own hours, so long as the work gets done.

- ❏ An opportunity to voice your opinion on critical issues.

- ❏ Creative control over a project.

- ❏ New responsibilities that you choose for yourself.

- ❏ The chance to telecommute one day a week so long as you remain productive.

- ❏ The opportunity to select your own professional development courses and seminars.

- ❏ The opportunity to train other employees.

- ❏ A story in the organization's newsletter about your valuable contribution.

- ❏ A certificate of achievement.

- ❏ An announcement of your accomplishment at a staff meeting.

- ❏ The "customer service champion" (or top sales producer, etc.) parking place for the next month.

- ❏ A sincere, hand-written note from your manager.

- ❏ Other _____

_____

Everyone can personalize the recognition they give. Leaders can assemble special teams to research recognition options for milestone events. Teams can ask members to share what forms of recognition they prefer, using the information to recognize each other. Individuals can observe their coworkers and learn what hobbies and other outside interests they have, using that information to thank each other or acknowledge their contribution. Managers can use any of these methods. They can also provide a more structured opportunity to discover their employees' preferences.

Managers and Supervisors Interview for Preference

If you are the manager or supervisor, you can use a preference interview to help you get to know employees better. The preference interview is nothing more than a structured conversation. Like the discussion about employee contribution, it can help you to build recognition into the work, creating more job satisfaction. You may find some overlap with the conversation about contribution, but not necessarily.

Begin the preference conversation by clarifying your purpose. Let the employee know that you want to ask a few questions in order to better understand what would make her work more enjoyable. Once the employee is comfortable with the purpose and process of the interview, you can begin. Listed below are some open-ended questions about preferences, along with some possible responses and hints on how the information might be used to recognize and motivate.

What do you love about your job?

Response 1: "I love that I can leave at 5:00 most evenings to be with my family." To keep this person happy and productive you shouldn't habitually ask them to stay late. Recognize and reward her with time off to be used at her discretion.

Response 2: "I love the independence that I have to do the job as I see fit." If the job is getting done satisfactorily, you will want to make sure this person remains unrestrained or unrestricted. This person will appreciate increased autonomy because it recognizes her ability to work independently.

Response 3: "I love solving a customer's problem and seeing the smile on his face when he leaves." Promoting this person to a position where interaction with other people is limited would probably damage her job satisfaction. It would be better to recognize her value by providing new opportunities to use her people skills and problem-solving abilities.

As your manager (or supervisor), what could I do to make your job more satisfying?

Response 1: "I would like you to help me prepare for a promotion." An excellent way to recognize this employee would be to introduce her to key managers, or provide a coach or needed training. Many managers would hesitate to groom valued employees for a promotion because they don't want to lose them. But if you get a reputation as someone who helps people advance their careers, you will usually find that many desirable candidates are waiting to take the departing employee's place.

Response 2: "You could provide more social opportunities for the department." This employee values the social bonding of the group. You can recognize her, by recognizing the department with impromptu pizza parties and team-building activities at meetings. This employee would probably also appreciate being put in charge of birthday celebrations.

Response 3: "You could let others know how hard I work, so they don't try to dump their stuff on me." This employee wants public recognition for her contribution. Based on the emotion evident in the response, there might be more going on here. You would want to explore this response further.

How would you like to be recognized?

It's better if you've learned the answer to this question during regular interactions with the employee, but if not, asking this question now will help you learn more about employee preferences. If the employee doesn't have any ideas, suggest a few manageable possibilities and see what she selects.

After the Interview

Immediately after the interview make a few notes about what you learned. Summarize how this information will help you personalize recognition. Over the next few months, as you begin to recognize employees, track the frequency, purpose, and form of recognition given as well as the employees' reactions. By reviewing this information frequently, you can consider the following questions and respond accordingly:

Has an employee gone unrecognized for more than a month?
- Many managers say they have employees who aren't doing anything that merits recognition. In most cases, they aren't paying close enough attention to employee performance, or they're setting their expectations too high. Most employees are doing something worth recognizing. If you have an employee whose performance is so poor that there is really nothing to recognize, you need to take the appropriate steps to let the employee go.
- The problem may be the way the employee responded to past recognition. If an award was met with an embarrassed silence or the employee seemed disappointed with a new opportunity, it is time to ask more questions. Discover whether the recognition itself was inappropriate, or if some other factor is at work. Adjust your recognition as necessary to accommodate employee preferences.
- Often managers simply forget to recognize employee performance. It's difficult to establish a new habit. You can get busy and forget. Make the effort to get into the recognition habit, because appreciation makes work flow more smoothly and people more

productive. Everything else becomes harder when you skip recognition. Skip recognition and you will spend more time dealing with employee dissatisfaction and higher turnover. Invest the time in recognizing employees and watch your job get easier.

Remember the Gallup survey: people want recognition at least every seven days. As the manager, don't feel you have to offer all the recognition yourself. Recognition should be coming from a variety of sources. To increase the amount of recognition each employee receives, you can enlist the help of other people. Just don't abdicate all responsibility. Remember that recognition from you is typically the most highly regarded recognition that your employees receive.

Is most of the recognition employees are receiving taking one form?

- Variety requires creativity (or some good resource books) and a quick review of employee preferences. When you review preferences, you may recall that one employee would like to take a class while another prefers lunch with you and a major client. Find ways to add variety while honoring employee preferences.

Recognition is an ongoing process. You need to follow up regularly with employees to see if your recognition efforts are on target. Talking about preferences will create the expectation of personalized recognition and will lead to disappointment if you don't deliver. Continue to learn more about your employees. Do they enjoy skiing, golfing, or photography? Do they like public recognition? Are silly awards fun or stupid? Use what you learn to tailor recognition. Recognize employees frequently and in a variety of appropriate ways.

Interview Everyone

Having a conversation with every employee is time-consuming. It is also worth every minute spent doing it. Whether you do a formal interview or have casual hallway discussions over the course of several months, the insights you gain and the loyalty you build will more than justify the time it takes.

Managers Aren't the Only Ones Who Can Discover Preferences

It is important to reiterate that everyone can individualize recognition. The time you spend learning about the people you work with is, in itself, a significant form of recognition. Regardless of whether you are a manager or supervisor—or a team member, cubicle mate, or internal customer—when you learn a little something about the people around you, they feel more valued. Learn what they like to do in their spare time, what they like to eat, or what kind of music they enjoy. Your interest and concern will positively impact those relationships and allow you to recognize people more appropriately.

Recognize Unique Contributions with Personalized Recognition

Once you know what people value, you can offer recognition that has specific meaning. You can recognize unique contributions with personalized rewards by doing two things.

First, when you give recognition, provide a complete description of the valued behavior or accomplishment and tell how it helps the group or organization.

> Years ago I received a regional customer service award from a company that I represented. The regional manager presented the award to me at the annual regional meeting with all of my peers in attendance. I didn't know ahead of time that I had won. The manager began the presentation

by reading the criteria for the award: consistent concern for customers, a high level of product knowledge, and a willingness to go the extra mile to ensure excellence in customer service. Then she read a lengthy client quote. At one point the quote became so specific I recognized the client and realized I was the winner. It was a very special moment. Fifteen years later the award still has significance for me. I knew what the company valued and knew someone had put a considerable amount of effort into verifying that I had met their standards. The detailed description of my contribution made the reward meaningful.

Second, offer recognition specifically selected for the recipient based on your knowledge of what they value. In my case, I enjoyed the public praise, so the award was a good choice. I like to think my representative knew me well enough to know this of me. Had I disliked public attention, I wouldn't have the same fond memory of this award.

What about the employee's family? Should you be able to safely acknowledge them without worrying about whether your recognition is personalized? It seems reasonable. After all, it's your job to know the employee, not their family—isn't it? Consider what the wife of a top salesperson shared regarding the recognition she received:

> "My husband's company sent me a big gift basket when he became the top salesman. I really resented that he had to work many overtime hours with no days off in order to make top salesman. I was actively lobbying to get him to change jobs at the time."

The fruit basket reminded the wife of all the hours her husband had spent away from the family. It had an impact, but not the one his company wanted. The person arranging for the basket assumed the salesman's family supported his long hours. Had this person known this salesman a little better, they could have made a better choice. A certificate for dinner for the family, along with a note of understanding, would have had a more positive impact.

Specific Contribution + Personalization = Meaningful Recognition

Consider a situation where someone adeptly facilitates the progress of a team meeting. You're a member of this team, though not necessarily the leader. You want to show your appreciation to the facilitator. If the facilitator appreciates public praise, the following might be an appropriate announcement.

> "This has been a productive meeting. Before we leave I want to acknowledge Mai for keeping us focused on the meeting's key objective—naming our new product. At one point we veered off into a discussion of product features. We made several other unintended 'detours,' and each time Mai brought us back to our objective tactfully but purposefully. Thank you Mai."

For a private person, this kind of public attention would be uncomfortable. Offer him the same message, one-to-one after the meeting, or send an e-mail message, possibly copying the other members of the team. Every person is different. One individual would like the opportunity to take a class. Another wants the chance to teach it. Make sure you know the preferences of the people you recognize.

Case Study—Recognition Misses the Mark

To test your ability to recognize individual preferences, try the following case study:

> April is in her midtwenties, single, friendly, but a little shy. She is a willing worker who accepts new challenges. She loves her job as a newspaper reporter. To see her name on

the byline of a hard news or human-interest story makes her day. Much of her job satisfaction comes from her belief that she makes a difference in the community where she works. She is also proud of the reputation of "her" paper in the community.

As much as April loves her work she also cherishes the time she has away from it. She has a close circle of friends who get together every Friday evening to cook a gourmet meal and talk about their week.

April's manager, Terrence, knows very little about April or what motivates her, but he does know that she will usually take on a challenge. A challenge is exactly what he has on his hands one Friday afternoon when the sportswriter goes home sick. Counting on April's willingness to pitch in, Terrence asks her to cover the football game at the local university that evening and have an article ready in the morning. April reluctantly agrees. She hurries her "real" news story and misses the Friday night dinner party. Saturday morning she turns in an excellent article.

At the Monday staff meeting, Terrence announces that they have a terrific new sportswriter on the team. He thinks he is offering positive recognition for April's accomplishment, but April is mortified. What went wrong? What could Terrence do differently?

Take a moment to go back through the story and note what April values and what forms of recognition she might prefer. Note what you discover.

What Went Wrong?

Terrence senses April is a team player who values her ability to contribute to the overall quality of the paper. He knows that she is usually up to a challenge and uses that knowledge to get her to take on the sports assignment. He knows enough about her to get her to do the work—at least one time.

To motivate April long-term, Terrence should take into account the following:

April:

- Is shy and doesn't want praise in front of her coworkers
- Doesn't want to do sports stories
- Prefers hard news and human-interest assignments
- Wants to make a difference in the community
- Has pride in the reputation of the paper in the community
- Values her time off to spend with friends
- Is interested in gourmet food
- Likes interesting challenges

April quickly discovers that Terrence is unaware of her interests and ambitions. She realizes he doesn't know what she values, or worse, doesn't care. Next time she'll be less willing to help out, and if it happens too many times, she will take her willingness to pitch in to another newspaper.

Getting it Right

Terrence could send her an e-mail, voice mail, or note recognizing her willingness to pitch in with quality work, even when the subject is one that doesn't interest her. That alone would go a long way with April. He could double the impact if he then rewarded her with any of the following:

- A choice assignment in either of her two areas of interest
- A gift certificate for her favorite restaurant or gourmet market
- A cooking lesson with a local chef

Like April, your people want personalized recognition. One-size-fits all recognition gives them the impression that you only care about their achievements. If you don't take their preferences into account, they will assume you don't care about them as people. Know what is important to them. Listen to what they have to say. Then recognize your people by giving them more of what they like and less of what they don't like. Give recognition that shows employees that they matter. Offer recognition that makes their day!

TAKING ACTION

- Learn more about the people around you. Find out what is important to them.
- Use what you learn to offer recognition that takes their interests and needs into account.

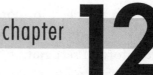

Recognition Is a Work in Progress

Effective Recognition Requires Both Commitment and Planning

There's no quick fix for poor morale and underappreciated employees. It requires time to create the kind of work environment where recognition is inherent and to build the kinds of relationships necessary to make recognition meaningful. Trust is established and relationships are built over the long term.

When any new initiative is introduced, most employees take a wait-and-see approach. Past experience has taught them not to get too excited until they see if management will really support the change. Employees will do the same thing when you begin to offer recognition. You will have to prove your commitment before they'll trust your approach.

Although the need for commitment may seem obvious, the importance of planning isn't as clear. You can offer reasonably effective informal recognition with little or no planning. A little commitment and a lot of sincerity can go a long way. But if you want to offer consistent, fair, and frequent recognition, it helps to have an implementation plan. Without a plan, recognition is likely to be sporadic and inconsistent.

Think of recognition as a long-term project. Successful projects require planning. This chapter will help you define the scope of your recognition project, assess your resources, define the limited scope of a pilot project, and put in place a process for continuous improvement.

Benefits of a Pilot Project

When many managers begin to offer recognition, there is a tendency to start too big. They roll out a full-scale program with lots of fanfare and then experience an unanticipated setback. After the setback, they find it's more difficult to stay committed and keep others committed to the process. It is likely that they will get discouraged and fail in their attempt to offer meaningful recognition.

Learning to offer effective recognition is a little like learning to juggle. Start by trying to juggle six balls at once, and you're sure to drop them all. It's better to start with one ball and learn proper form and timing before increasing the number of balls you try to keep in the air. Learning to juggle in this manner may not seem exciting, but you'll be more competent, and people will have more confidence in your capabilities as a juggler if you do.

Using a recognition pilot project is a little like juggling a single ball. It's a manageable opportunity to work on technique and form, make adjustments, and become competent. The recognition pilot project gives you a chance to become skilled at juggling one ball before you pick up another. In the process, it decreases the likelihood that you will drop the ball.

Pilot projects provide an excellent opportunity to evaluate what works well, uncover potential problems, and make sure resources are used effectively. They can also be used to make recognition more effective. FedEx Freight tests their safety recognition programs by rolling them out to a single division. Containing the program within a single division allows FedEx Freight to compare the safety records of that division with the other divisions. This restriction helps clarify the impact of the new program. FedEx Freight uses the pilot to ask questions, assess results, and make improvements.

A well-designed pilot project can also generate buy-in. If you are developing an organization-wide program, and some managers show reluctance or lack the necessary recognition skills, begin the pilot with a manager who is capable and enthusiastic. The goal is to choose someone who is likely to be successful. When other managers see the resulting positive changes in employee attitude and performance, they will be more interested in becoming involved. When employees see others being recognized in a meaningful way, they will also be more enthusiastic. Success breeds success.

Start Small, Evaluate, and Adjust

The principles of a pilot project work just as well for individual managers and supervisors as they do for organization-wide recognition programs. The basic steps still apply: start small, evaluate, and adjust. A supervisor who wants to begin recognizing employees might start by sending everyone a hand-written note outlining what each individual has done to support the team. Then, by gauging reactions and making adjustments, he can improve his ability to offer effective recognition. The supervisor then repeats the cycle, adding another form of recognition or increasing the frequency. By progressing slowly, he keeps recognition and expectations at a manageable level. This supervisor will have more success doing less than he would have if he set expectations too high and then failed to deliver.

To limit the scope of a pilot project, consider the following restrictions:

- The number of people involved. Choose a single team or department so that you will be able to compare results.
- The form recognition takes. Focus your pilot project on selecting appropriate development opportunities, or simply saying thank-you. Be sure that you are really recognizing the person and her achievements and are taking her personal preferences into account.
- The frequency of recognition. If recognition is a new habit, remembering to recognize every employee just once a month will be a challenge. Develop consistency before trying to increase frequency.

The Three-Step Recognition Process

Whether you are a supervisor looking for ways to acknowledge the accomplishments of your direct reports, an employee charged with developing a recognition idea for your department, or a director of Human Resources charged with setting up a full-scale recognition program, it's best to use this three-step process.

Step one: Determine the current state of recognition. On a large scale, this assessment is done with employee surveys followed by focus groups or one-on-one interviews. On a small scale, a few discussions with key employees will provide a fairly clear picture of what is going on and show which improvements will have the most immediate impact.

Step two: Plan your recognition strategy. For bigger projects, planning your strategy means identifying resources and setting your budget, goals, and deadlines. On a much smaller scale, it might mean deciding how frequently you are going to personally thank each person.

Step three: Commit to a long-term, graduated implementation. No matter what the size of your recognition effort, implementing recognition needs to be an ongoing cycle: implement, observe, evaluate the results, and then adapt and improve as you start the whole process again.

Step One: Determine the Current State of Recognition

Chefs taste the food as they prepare a meal. They don't add more seasoning without first sampling the flavor of the dish. If they did, they might end up adding too much salt or spice to a dish that is already salty or spicy enough. They taste the food because they want to know how existing flavors are working together. Tasting helps them to figure out what is missing or how they can best complement what they already have.

The same principle works with employee recognition. Before you decide what would be complementary or what needs to change, you need to determine what you already have. You need to figure out what's working and what's not. To establish a starting point, assess your employees' satisfaction with existing recognition.

Job Satisfaction Surveys

As you've worked your way through this book, you will have discovered that many of the things that positively influence job satisfaction contain one or more of the elements of recognition. Because recognition and job satisfaction are so closely intertwined, measuring job satisfaction can be an excellent gauge of the effectiveness of recognition. To measure job satisfaction you can purchase a standard job satisfaction survey or create your own.

FedEx Freight has generously allowed reprinting of their Employee Quality of Worklife Survey.[1] This survey is a good example of a general job satisfaction survey. FedEx Freight uses job, location, and department categories to help identify where job satisfaction excels and where it lags behind. In order to give you a sense of the breakdown FedEx Freight uses, you will find a partial list of their categories.

The FedEx survey measures job satisfaction. You can also measure for recognition satisfaction specifically. Use the recognition survey that follows the FedEx Freight survey. Although it won't give as comprehensive a view of job satisfaction, it does provide a more in-depth look at recognition satisfaction.

FedEx Freight Employee Quality of Worklife Survey 2000

Service Center/Maintenance/Field Sales

Place an ☑ in the appropriate job classification box
and another ☑ in the appropriate location box

❏ Maintenance   ❏ Hostler/Fueler   ❏ Dockworker
❏ Field Salesperson   ❏ Linehaul Driver   ❏ Ops
❏ Field Sales Clerical ❏ Local/P&D Driver   ❏ Ops Supervisor

❏ Alaska   ❏ Las Vegas
❏ Albuquerque   ❏ Phoenix
❏ Bend   ❏ Pocatello
❏ Boise   ❏ Portland
❏ Chico   ❏ Reno
❏ Colorado Springs   ❏ Sacramento
❏ Denver   ❏ Salem
❏ El Paso   ❏ Salt Lake City
❏ Eugene   ❏ San Diego
❏ Eureka   ❏ San Fernando Valley
❏ Flagstaff   ❏ San Luis Obispo
❏ Gardena   ❏ Seattle
❏ Hawaii   ❏ Tacoma
❏ Huntington Park   ❏ Tucson
❏ Kingman   ❏ Twin Falls

General Office/Administrative Departments/CAS

Place an ☑ in the appropriate department box

❏ Accounting
❏ Credit & Collections & Invoicing
❏ Cash Application, Error Controls
❏ Central Line Control
❏ Claims
❏ Claims Prevention
❏ OPS Planning & Engineering
❏ Customer Service
❏ Customer Mgmt & Switchboard – San Jose
❏ Customer Billing Assurance
❏ Human Resources
❏ Info Technology
❏ Inside Sales
❏ Market Analysis
❏ Corporate Communications
❏ Product Marketing
❏ Corporate Account Sales

FedEx Freight Employee Quality of Worklife Survey 2000, Continued

Circle the answer that best describes your feelings

	STRONGLY AGREE	AGREE	NEITHER AGREE NOR DISAGREE	DISAGREE	STRONGLY DISAGREE
1. When I arrive at work, I feel welcome.	YES	yes	neither	no	NO
2. I enjoy my job and the work I do.	YES	yes	neither	no	NO
3. I have a clear understanding of what's expected of me at work.	YES	yes	neither	no	NO
4. I feel a sense of control over my day-to-day work activities.	YES	yes	neither	no	NO
5. I feel appreciated for a job well done.	YES	yes	neither	no	NO
6. I am respected and I feel like part of a family.	YES	yes	neither	no	NO
7. I am proud to be part of FedEx Freight.	YES	yes	neither	no	NO
8. I am paid fairly compared with other FedEx Freight employees.	YES	yes	neither	no	NO
9. My total compensation compares favorably to similar jobs at other companies.	YES	yes	neither	no	NO
10. My supervisor is interested in my suggestions and ideas.	YES	yes	neither	no	NO
11. I have many opportunities to express my concerns to my supervisor.	YES	yes	neither	no	NO

FedEx Freight Employee Quality of Worklife Survey 2000, Continued

Circle the answer that best describes your feelings

	STRONGLY AGREE	AGREE	NEITHER AGREE NOR DISAGREE	DISAGREE	STRONGLY DISAGREE
12. My supervisor recognizes and rewards hard work and extra effort.	YES	yes	neither	no	NO
13. My supervisor keeps me informed about matters that effect me.	YES	yes	neither	no	NO
14. My supervisor supports me in my efforts to work safely.	YES	yes	neither	no	NO
15. My supervisor is approachable, easy to talk with.	YES	yes	neither	no	NO
16. My supervisor listens to my concerns and responds quickly.	YES	yes	neither	no	NO
17. FedEx Freight's work rules and policies are fair.	YES	yes	neither	no	NO
18. FedEx Freight's safety programs are effective.	YES	yes	neither	no	NO
19. FedEx Freight provides good benefits, health insurance, vacations, etc.	YES	yes	neither	no	NO
20. The President and Vice Presidents are interested in my suggestions and ideas.	YES	yes	neither	no	NO
21. The President and Vice Presidents are approachable, easy to talk with.	YES	yes	neither	no	NO
22. FedEx Freight is a better place to work than other trucking companies.	YES	yes	neither	no	NO
23. During the past year, I have recommended FedEx Freight as a place to work.	YES	yes	neither	no	NO
24. I have thought about leaving FedEx Freight because of unfair treatment on the job.	YES	yes	neither	no	NO

How can FedEx Freight improve as a place to work or as an industry leader? (include additional sheets if needed)

Recognition Survey

Circle the answer that best describes your feelings

1. I feel appreciated for a job well done.

   STRONGLY   NEITHER AGREE   STRONGLY
   AGREE   AGREE   NOR DISAGREE   DISAGREE   DISAGREE

2. My opinions matter to the people I work with.

   STRONGLY   NEITHER AGREE   STRONGLY
   AGREE   AGREE   NOR DISAGREE   DISAGREE   DISAGREE

3. My supervisor respects my judgment.

   STRONGLY   NEITHER AGREE   STRONGLY
   AGREE   AGREE   NOR DISAGREE   DISAGREE   DISAGREE

4. My supervisor recognizes me for my hard work.

   STRONGLY   NEITHER AGREE   STRONGLY
   AGREE   AGREE   NOR DISAGREE   DISAGREE   DISAGREE

5. I know what our organization values.

   STRONGLY   NEITHER AGREE   STRONGLY
   AGREE   AGREE   NOR DISAGREE   DISAGREE   DISAGREE

6. My work contributes to our goals and strategies.

   STRONGLY   NEITHER AGREE   STRONGLY
   AGREE   AGREE   NOR DISAGREE   DISAGREE   DISAGREE

7. My contributions are recognized in a way that reinforces the goals and
   strategies of the organization.

   STRONGLY   NEITHER AGREE   STRONGLY
   AGREE   AGREE   NOR DISAGREE   DISAGREE   DISAGREE

8. I know what is expected from me.

   STRONGLY   NEITHER AGREE   STRONGLY
   AGREE   AGREE   NOR DISAGREE   DISAGREE   DISAGREE

9. My supervisor works with me to develop my individual goals.

   STRONGLY   NEITHER AGREE   STRONGLY
   AGREE   AGREE   NOR DISAGREE   DISAGREE   DISAGREE

10. Recognition reinforces my individual work goals.

    STRONGLY   NEITHER AGREE   STRONGLY
    AGREE   AGREE   NOR DISAGREE   DISAGREE   DISAGREE

11. My supervisor knows and cares about what is important to me.

    STRONGLY   NEITHER AGREE   STRONGLY
    AGREE   AGREE   NOR DISAGREE   DISAGREE   DISAGREE

12. Quality is valued within my work group.

    STRONGLY   NEITHER AGREE   STRONGLY
    AGREE   AGREE   NOR DISAGREE   DISAGREE   DISAGREE

Recognition Survey, Continued

13. I receive some sort of praise or recognition every week.

| STRONGLY AGREE | AGREE | NEITHER AGREE NOR DISAGREE | DISAGREE | STRONGLY DISAGREE |

14. My coworkers appreciate my contribution.

| STRONGLY AGREE | AGREE | NEITHER AGREE NOR DISAGREE | DISAGREE | STRONGLY DISAGREE |

15. The company recognizes both teams and individuals for their contributions.

| STRONGLY AGREE | AGREE | NEITHER AGREE NOR DISAGREE | DISAGREE | STRONGLY DISAGREE |

16. I receive appropriate opportunities for growth and development.

| STRONGLY AGREE | AGREE | NEITHER AGREE NOR DISAGREE | DISAGREE | STRONGLY DISAGREE |

17. We have regular opportunities for fun at work.

| STRONGLY AGREE | AGREE | NEITHER AGREE NOR DISAGREE | DISAGREE | STRONGLY DISAGREE |

18. I know how to offer recognition to my coworkers.

| STRONGLY AGREE | AGREE | NEITHER AGREE NOR DISAGREE | DISAGREE | STRONGLY DISAGREE |

19. My coworkers know how to acknowledge my contributions.

| STRONGLY AGREE | AGREE | NEITHER AGREE NOR DISAGREE | DISAGREE | STRONGLY DISAGREE |

20. The recognition I receive is appropriate for me.

| STRONGLY AGREE | AGREE | NEITHER AGREE NOR DISAGREE | DISAGREE | STRONGLY DISAGREE |

21. The most deserving groups and individuals are usually recognized for their contributions.

| STRONGLY AGREE | AGREE | NEITHER AGREE NOR DISAGREE | DISAGREE | STRONGLY DISAGREE |

22. My supervisor knows and respects me.

| STRONGLY AGREE | AGREE | NEITHER AGREE NOR DISAGREE | DISAGREE | STRONGLY DISAGREE |

23. Awards and incentives reinforce high performance.

| STRONGLY AGREE | AGREE | NEITHER AGREE NOR DISAGREE | DISAGREE | STRONGLY DISAGREE |

24. My supervisor sets a good example for how we should acknowledge each other.

| STRONGLY AGREE | AGREE | NEITHER AGREE NOR DISAGREE | DISAGREE | STRONGLY DISAGREE |

Notice that some of the statements on the recognition survey look at recognition in terms of general appreciation, appreciation from a supervisor or manager, or appreciation among coworkers. Other statements look at recognition as a natural outcome of quality work. Others consider whether recognition is fair and frequent, or whether appropriate behavior is being modeled.

If you have existing recognition programs, be sure to assess those as well. Add your own statements to the survey. You might use statements such as, "The peer-nominated Customer Service Champion Award usually identifies the most deserving recipient," or "Employee Appreciation Day is a worthwhile recognition opportunity." The responses you receive will provide a good indication of the effectiveness of your programs.

Analyzing the Results

After you select and administer your survey, you need to interpret the results. You will discover areas of concern and reason for celebration. When you know what works best, you can build upon your successes. When you discover where problems exist, you will be able to take corrective action. Keep in mind that, often, instead of providing answers, surveys just create more questions. After your survey, ask yourself what the results mean. If only 25 percent of employees believe they get appropriate recognition, why is that true? Did respondents understand the statement as it was intended? Can they tell you what would make recognition more appropriate? To find the answers, follow up with one-on-one interviews. In order to see if participants understood and responded accordingly, it's appropriate to select employees randomly for follow-up. Random selection also works when low scores are representative of the entire group. But if a particular department or location is far below the standard score on a particular item, it is necessary to target individuals from that department or location for follow-up interviews.

Don't make assumptions about what the survey results mean. Follow up until you have a complete understanding of why respondents answered the way they did. Without thorough follow-up, you're likely to misinterpret the results.

Consider one consulting firm's satisfaction survey that included these three statements related to recognition.

(1) Teams are recognized for their contributions to improving how we work.

Eighty-two percent responded favorably to this statement, a good response.

(2) Individuals are recognized for their contributions to improving how we work.

Seventy-six percent responded favorably, still a pretty good rating.

(3) How satisfied are you with the recognition you get?

Only 56 percent responded favorably to this statement. This low response rate should have been a red flag for the firm. The burning question should have been *why* are only 56 percent of respondents satisfied with the recognition they get? The people analyzing the consulting firm's results assumed this question scored low because of a compensation and benefits issue. Their assumption may have been true, but because most employees don't consider compensation and benefits to be recognition, it's very likely that the firm's assumption was wrong. Without follow-up conversations or a new survey to separate recognition from compensation and benefits, they will never know for sure.

Forty-four percent of their employees expected to be recognized more effectively. Unless this firm finds out why these employees are dissatisfied, they aren't likely to improve the rating. If anything, people will become more dissatisfied because the survey raised their expectation for change and then change didn't occur.

Remember that the survey rarely provides answers. It creates more questions, questions that require further exploration.

Tips for surveying employees

- Keep your survey short, simple, and easy to complete and return.
- Work toward a high response rate. Consider passing out the survey at an employee meeting and asking employees to return the completed form before they leave.
- Ensure that responses are anonymous. Results will be more accurate if individuals know that their supervisors won't be able to identify them.
- Make supervisors accountable for their department's results. Accountability requires that you have a way to track responses to a specific supervisor. In most cases, you can track responses to their department without compromising the anonymity of individuals.
- Don't survey unless you intend to take action on the results. Surveying employees sets the expectation that something will change.
- Avoid making assumptions. Follow up with respondents to provide clarity and detail to your analysis.
- Use the results of your survey as an opportunity to initiate discussions that will develop a clear picture of what employees want and need.
- Don't use a survey to gauge the opinion of just a few people. If you are responsible for recognizing less than fifteen people, have a personal conversation with each one.
- Use the information you gather as the foundation for Step Two.

Step Two: Plan Your Recognition Strategy

Use what you learn about the current state of recognition in your organization or department as the basis for your recognition strategy.

Imagine you're the manager of a department of thirty people. You do a survey and discover that only 25 percent of your employees believe they get appropriate recognition. Further probing uncovers dissatisfaction with two company-sponsored programs. It seems no one is very happy with the monogrammed notepads the company gives out after ten years of dedicated service and most people think five-dollar gift certificates are an inappropriate way to acknowledge people whose suggestions lead to major cost-saving improvements.

Further discussion reveals that employees would like to choose their own rewards. As the manager, you know that you can opt out of these two company-sponsored programs if you choose. You can use your portion of the very meager recognition budget as you see fit. You wonder if it's possible to make better use of the limited funds available.

You begin to assess the rest of your resources. Talking to employees, you discover that your whole department is eager to get involved in the recognition process. You ask for volunteers for a recognition planning team and set a goal to repeat the survey in four months to see if the team can achieve 75 percent satisfaction.

The first thing the team does is to confirm your decision to scrap the notepads and certificates. They decide, with the current budget limitations, meaningful individual rewards aren't possible. The team thinks it would be more fun to use the money for an auction. You ask how an auction will provide recognition. The team leader explains that the auction will be based around a peer-recognition program. The team plans to print "Thanks for . . ." cards. Everyone in the department will receive a supply of the cards to use to recognize their coworkers. The cards will have space for the giver to describe what they are saying "Thanks for . . ." The cards will also have a tear-off stub for recipients to use as a token for bidding in the quarterly auction.

The team plans to use the entire recognition budget for printing and auction items, so they decide to ask each employee to bring a favorite food to share on the day of the auction. This way they can add to the fun with a celebratory lunch. You offer to act as master of ceremony for the event and plan to use the opportunity to express your own words of appreciation.

Identify Resources

Before you decide what you are going to do, you need to know what resources you have to work with. As the the last example shows, your resources will include both your budget and the people who can assist you. You don't need a lot of money. You can even provide great recognition with no money at all. Still, you will be more effective if you know what you have to work with and plan for how it will be used.

In the example, your team knew their budget and planned for its use. Consider another example where the manager doesn't plan ahead.

Your manager begins her own recognition program. The first time she recognizes you, it is for getting your status reports from the last twelve months in on time and error-free. As a reward, you receive an overnight trip for two to the city. You think, "Wow, this is great!" Your manager provides a number of people in your department with similar rewards. She also offers her sincere appreciation for a job well-done.

The next time she recognizes you, it is for mentoring another supervisor. Along with your manager's praise, you receive two movie passes. You are confused; you were sure your manager valued the mentoring you provided more than your timely, error-free status reports. So you wonder,

"Am I inadequate as a mentor? Is mentoring really as important as I thought?" Throughout the rest of year, you continue to receive your share of praise and thank-yous, but no additional rewards, even though you do some remarkable work. You continue to have doubts about what your manager values and the quality of your work.

In this example, you didn't know your manager depleted her recognition budget early in the year. Although she continued to offer you quality recognition, the accompanying rewards were inconsistent. That inconsistency led to confusion. The rewards that were supposed to reinforce recognition only served to muddy it.

Without some sense of what you can spend, there is a tendency to use up a large portion of available funds early on and then fall back on free recognition. Employee expectations are set in the early stages, so when rewards diminish over time, it creates confusion and disappointment. You want to use the highest-value awards to recognize the highest-value accomplishments, and you want to present some awards later in the year in order to maintain excitement. The only way you can do this is with planning.

What if you have no budget for recognition and aren't likely to get one? In most cases you can still find money for recognition. Often, with a little creativity, you can make the line items on your budget serve double-duty.

A large professional association with no budget for recognition has budgeted for a monthly member newsletter. The director decides to add a regular feature to this newsletter. It will highlight a different employee each month, describing the employee's job function, interests, and contribution to the association. Members will benefit from the addition because they will learn more about the people who work on their behalf. Employees will benefit from much-needed recognition.

When you look for money for recognition, look for funds that can serve two purposes. Some sources to consider include funds set-aside for bonuses, employee events or celebrations, training, or the manager's discretionary use. These funds can provide additional opportunities for recognition. Make them serve both their intended purpose and your recognition strategy.

Set Realistic Goals and Time Frames

In the auction example, you set a goal to repeat the survey in four months and show an improvement from 25 percent to 75 percent. Can you achieve this goal? Possibly, but it probably isn't very realistic to expect that kind of improvement from one peer recognition program. A better goal would be 50 percent.

Is the four-month deadline realistic? To see if it is, identify smaller goals or phases, and estimate the time it will take to complete each. Your team decides the following are the critical phases, and estimates the time each will take.

Phase 1—Designing and printing the cards—four weeks.
Phase 2—Developing and communicating criteria—three weeks.
Phase 3—Running the card program—three months.
Phase 4—Selecting auction items—two weeks.
Phase 5—Planning a celebration—one week.
Phase 6—Holding the auction and celebration—two hours.

If you total the time required, it would add up to approximately six months. But this doesn't take into account that many of these phases can happen concurrently. The people on your team can complete the first two phases at the same time, so the card program can begin in four weeks. Phases 4 and 5 can both take place while the card program is running. You will be ready to hold the auction and resurvey your department in four months—right on schedule.

Step Three: Commit to a Continually Evolving Implementation

Recognition works best when you start small, gain competence and confidence, and then slowly expand your efforts. Employees respond favorably when they see that recognition isn't a flavor-of-the-week initiative. Step Three in the process creates a cycle of continuous improvement that makes recognition most effective: implement, observe, evaluate, and improve.

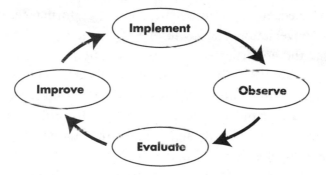

Implement

With your project plan in place, you are ready to begin the implementation. Complete the steps as you have planned them. As you implement, don't forget to communicate your recognition plan to those who are involved. Communicating your plan isn't as important with informal recognition, but if you are planning a formal program it becomes critical. It is very important that you provide adequate information about what they can expect from your program. Describe the kind of recognition you'll be offering and what you're looking for in terms of behavior and accomplishment. If your surveys and questionnaires uncovered recognition problems, acknowledge these and describe how you plan to remedy them. Invite employees to offer feedback as the implementation proceeds. To improve the odds of long-term success, encourage open communication throughout the process.

Observe and Evaluate

Observe what works and what doesn't. Evaluate the results of your efforts. The question to ask is, "Are we having the impact that we want to have?" If the answer is no, you need to know why.

> A vice president expressed to me that while he showed appreciation and recognized his employees, no one ever reciprocated. He said employees were quick to bring him their complaints when he didn't deliver, but they never acknowledged any improvement in *his* performance. In a later conversation I had with one of his managers, we discussed the importance of "recognizing up." The manager told me his VP didn't like compliments. He said he had attempted to acknowledge his VP during a meeting and observed that the VP was clearly uncomfortable. I asked him to consider that it might not be the compliment, but something else that had made the VP uncomfortable. He decided to try a different forum for offering appreciation. After our conversation, he sent the VP an e-mail thanking him for his help on a recent project and received back a very positive response.

Observe how people respond to the recognition you give. Use follow-up discussions and surveys to gain more information. Look at people's reaction to recognition, but also consider other factors. Have attitudes changed? Are people more productive and self-directed? In evaluating your success, also consider the changes recognition may have had on your operations. The same measures you used to track achievement will help you evaluate the impact of recognition on your operations. With measures in place, you will be able to determine whether costs, safety violations, or the number of sick days taken have decreased. You will be able to show whether outcomes such as productivity, percentage of repeat business, or the close rate on leads have increased.

It is likely that only a percentage of the changes you measure will be attributable to your recognition efforts. You may be wondering, "Exactly how much impact did recognition have?" It can be hard to tell, but if you use a pilot project, those people who aren't included in the pilot offer a reasonably good comparison. By comparing the results of the two groups, you can start to separate the impact of recognition from the other factors that may have influenced the measurements.

Compare where you were before to where you are now. The information you gather will help you to figure out what is working and what can be improved. It will help to give your recognition greater impact.

Improve

Now that you have analyzed and clarified your results, you can identify your strengths and weaknesses. Congratulate yourself on what you have accomplished so far. Build on your strengths. Figure out what you can do to improve.

After completing the auction project mentioned earlier, you survey your department to find you have 45 percent employee satisfaction. That is an improvement of 20 percent—good progress—but still far from being an excellent rating. You look for ways to improve it. Further discussions with employees reveal that while they like the peer-recognition program, they want more recognition directly from you, the manager.

As you begin the cycle of improvement, you set a new goal—65 percent satisfaction at the end of the next three months. Your plan: continue the "Thanks for . . ." cards, have a conversation with each employee in order to learn more about their personal preferences, and use that knowledge to individualize recognition. You commit to personally recognizing every employee at least twice during the next three months. To complete the cycle you implement your plan, observe and evaluate the results, and make the necessary changes so you can continue to improve.

Where Do You Go from Here?

Employees crave meaningful recognition. When they talk about the recognition they receive, they're talking about how valued they feel. In order to help the people you work with to feel valued, you need to focus on the essence of what recognition is. Instead of offering recognition at a superficial level, you need to remember to look at recognition in the bigger context and the long term. Recognition isn't a plaque; it's the meaning behind the plaque. It's about building relationships and taking a personal, genuine interest in people and their preferences. So long as you do that and continue to look for ways to refine the recognition that you offer—employees will feel recognized. That, in turn, will improve morale, productivity, and profitability—and everybody wins.

TAKING ACTION

- Commit to a long-term solution to your employees' recognition needs.
- Take on only as much as you can accomplish successfully.
- Ask questions. Learn what is working and what isn't.
- Plan carefully and act consistently.
- Reap the rewards of recognition that works!

Books

The following are just a few of the books that will help you create the kind of work environment where employees feel recognized. Some focus on inherent recognition, some provide fun ideas that will spur your creativity, and others teach the specifics of goal-setting and measurement—important elements of recognition.

The Arbinger Institute. *Leadership and Self-Deception: Getting Out of the Box*. San Francisco: Berrett-Koehler, 2002.

Blanchard, Kenneth H., and Sheldon Bowles. *Gung Ho!: Turn On the People in Any Organization*. New York: William Morrow and Co., 1998.

Buckingham, Marcus, and Curt Coffman. *First, Break All the Rules: What the World's Greatest Managers Do Differently*. New York: Simon & Schuster, 1999.

Catlette, Bill, and Richard Hadden. *Contented Cows Give Better Milk: The Plain Truth About Employee Relations and Your Bottom Line*. Germantown, Tenn.: Saltillo Press, 2001.

Hemsath, Dave. *301 More Ways to Have Fun at Work*. San Francisco: Berrett-Koehler, 2001.

— —, and Leslie Yerkes. *301 Ways to Have Fun at Work*. San Francisco: Berrett-Koehler, 1997.

Kaye. Beverly L.. and Sharon Jordan-Evans. *Love 'Em or Lose 'Em: Getting Good People to Stay.* San Francisco: Berrett-Koehler, 1999.

Kouzes, James M., and Barry Z. Posner. *Encouraging the Heart: A Leader's Guide to Rewarding and Recognizing Others.* San Francisco: Jossey-Bass, 1999.

Nelson, Bob. *1001 Ways to Energize Employees.* New York: Workman Publishing, 1997.

———. *1001 Ways to Reward Employees.* New York: Workman Publishing, 1994.

———, and Dean Spitzer. *1001 Rewards & Recognition Fieldbook.* New York: Workman Publishing, 2002.

Niven, Paul R. *Balanced Scorecard Step-by-Step: Maximizing Performance and Maintaining Results.* New York: John Wiley & Sons, 2002.

Smith, Douglas K. *Make Success Measurable!: A Mindbook-Workbook for Setting Goals and Taking Action.* New York: John Wiley & Sons, 1999.

Thomas, Kenneth W. *Intrinsic Motivation at Work: Building Energy & Commitment.* San Francisco: Berrett-Koehler, 2000.

Web Sites

The following are just a few of the Web sites that will provide more information about employee recognition.

www.bluemountain.com One of many on-line, animated greeting card Web sites. It has a career-related section and more general thank-you cards. For a listing of other greeting card sites, search on *virtual greeting cards*.

www.beyondwork.com Their Giftpass program is an on-line gift certificate program with easy-to-use software for tracking usage and adjusting payroll. For other similar programs, search on *employee gift certificate programs*.

www.maketheirday.com For the latest recognition-related information and to contact the author regarding speaking engagements, workshops, or book purchases.

www.recognition.org The Web site for the National Association for Employee Recognition. They provide a forum for information and best practices around recognition.

www.robbins.com A source for high-quality awards that also provides program development and administration for *Fortune 500* clients. For other sites with related products and services, search on *employee awards and gifts*.

Preface

1. It's difficult to differentiate money spent on recognition from that spent on incentives. Stolovich, Clark, and Condly, authors of *Incentive, Motivation and Workplace Performance: Research and Best Practices*, estimate $117 billion are spent on incentives, including variable pay. My far more conservative $18 billion estimate for both incentives (excluding variable pay) and recognition is based on the following data. The National Association of Employee Recognition estimates $2 billion is spent on trophies, plaques, and other engravable awards. "The Incentive Merchandise and Travel Marketplace 2000" study estimates $12 billion is spent each year on travel, merchandise, and gift certificates. No figures were available on cash awards, such as spot bonuses and team awards, so I estimated a very conservative $4 billion.

2. For the four quarters ending June 2002, Hasbro reported $2.88 billion in revenue, and Yahoo! reported $773 million. For the four quarters ending May 2002, Nike reported $12.38 billion.

3. The National Association of Employee Recognition and WorldatWork reported, in a joint survey completed in 2001, that 86 percent of respondents had a recognition program in place.

4. Kepner-Tregoe, in their 1995 study "People and Their Jobs," found that only 40 percent of workers say they are rewarded or recognized by their supervisor.

5. When I began teaching a course on overcoming burnout, I started asking employees about recognition they received and what kind of recognition they wanted to receive. Their stories gave me my first glimpse at what really matters in terms of recognition. Later I asked the members of several on-line communities to share their stories of recognition, particularly recognition that had made a lasting impact. They responded in force, some referring me to others who had stories they thought I should hear. I continued to ask workshop

participants to tell their stories. Once the word got out that I wanted to hear about meaningful recognition, the stories began coming from all directions. It seemed that everyone who learned of my interest had a story to tell. I continued to gather stories at seminars and workshops, in my clients' places of business, in coffee shops, and once even in the ladies' room. Even those who provided a critique of this book's rough draft frequently started out by saying, "First, I want you to hear my story."

Introduction

1. Bob Tagg, Director Customer Support Americas at Remedy, reported Remedy statistics on layoffs and customer satisfaction and revenue.
2. Revenue overstatement and resignations reported May 6, 2002, by United Press International.
3. Peregrine Systems notified of NASDAQ intent to delist. AP Worldstream, June 27, 2002.
4. Bob Tagg.

Chapter 1

1. Bob Nelson, *1001 Ways to Reward Employees* (New York: Workman Publishing, 1994)
2. Dave Hemsath and Leslie Yerkes, *301 Ways to Have Fun at Work* (San Francisco: Berrett-Koehler Publishers, 1997)

Chapter 2

1. There is an ongoing debate whether external motivators or incentives work. Alfie Kohn has written many books and articles on the topic, including the book *Punished By Rewards* and an article for the *Harvard Business Review*, "Why Incentive Plans Cannot Work." In contrast, Harold Stolovitch, Richard Clark, and Steven Condly did a meta-analysis of all the research on the topic. They found that incentives positively and strongly influence performance. Their findings, "Incentive, Motivation and Workplace Performance: Research and Best Practices," are available through the Professional Society for Performance Improvement.

2. David C. McClelland, *The Achievement Motive* (New York: Appleton-Century Crofts, 1953); *Power: The Inner Experience* (New York: Irvington Publishers, 1975)
3. Lorraine Monroe, *Nothing's Impossible: Leadership Lessons from Inside the Classroom.* (New York: Public Affairs, 1997)
4. "Rewards of Work 2000," a study conducted jointly by Worldat-Work and Nextera's Sibson Consulting Group, identified five areas of focus for employee retention and motivation: career opportunities, feedback from the supervisor, job security, satisfaction with job title, and training and development opportunities. Career opportunities had the lowest satisfaction rate.
5. In *The Motivation to Work* (1959), Fredrick Herzberg established his hygiene theory that said that certain factors such as working conditions, salary, and benefits aren't motivators, but the lack of these factors leads to employee dissatisfaction.

Chapter 3

1. Steven Covey talks about the emotional bank account in his book *The Seven Habits of Highly Effective People* (New York: Simon & Schuster, 1990).
2. The name of the award was changed to allow for the director's anonymity.

Chapter 4

1. Maritz Research of Fenton, Missouri. The survey included one thousand employees.

Chapter 9

1. Heritage Award information provided with permission of Mike Slette, Director of Human Resources, Microsoft Great Plains Software.
2. "How Dell Keeps from Stumbling," *Business Week*, May 14, 2001.
3. Marcus Buckingham and Curt Coffman, *First, Break All the Rules: What the World's Greatest Managers Do Differently* (New York: Simon and Schuster, 1999).

4. Douglas K. Smith, *Make Success Measurable!: A Mindbook-Workbook for Setting Goals and Taking Action* (New York: John Wiley & Sons, 1999).

Chapter 10

1. *The Toastmaster* reported in its October 2000 issue that the Grand Pioneer club in Amherst, New York, had developed The Terrific Toastmaster Award as a way to encourage leadership among its members.

Chapter 11

1. Peter Drucker, *Management Challenges for the 21st Century* (New York: Harper Business, 1999).

Chapter 12

1. The Quality of Worklife survey is provided with the permission of Tom Suchevits, Vice President of Human Resources, FedEx Freight West.

Cindy Ventrice is a management consultant and workshop leader with nearly twenty years of experience. Through her company, Potential Unlimited, she has spent the last six years helping organizations improve performance by improving working relationships. She has been very active in the American Society for Training and Development, serving on the board of the Silicon Valley chapter since January 2000 and as chapter President in 2003.

Upon graduation from college in 1983, Cindy was employed in the fledgling personal computer field as a special projects manager. After only six months, her employer went bankrupt and laid off its entire work force. The contacts she made during this brief employment allowed her to leverage her knowledge of computer systems and establish herself as an independent consultant. In that capacity, she helped hundreds of organizations computerize their accounting and operational systems, acting as advisor, project manager, technical resource, and trainer.

Her strong understanding of technology provided Cindy with an opportunity to work on many diverse projects including:

developing bakery production and real estate management systems, and setting up job-costing, inventory tracking, payroll pro-
cessing, and point-of-sale systems. Over time she had the
opportunity to work in a wide range of industries including: technology, nonprofit, government, healthcare, manufacturing, trade,
service, education, and tourism, developing a comprehensive
understanding of business operations.

With each project, Cindy had a chance to observe and learn,
firsthand, about employee loyalty and motivation. She began to see
a correlation between project success and the way employees are
treated, and eventually she developed a project management course
that focused less on scheduling and resource management and
more on the cooperative and collaborative elements of effective
project management.

Slowly she moved away from technology-based solutions and
toward people-based solutions, creating a variety of workshops
solidly grounded in basic business operations. One workshop
taught companies how to maneuver through the risks associated
with organizational change. Another taught managers how to get
employees excited about improving customer service.

Today Cindy's consulting practice focuses exclusively on helping organizations improve operations, products, and services by
improving workplace relationships and employee morale. She
works with organizations in both the public and private sectors,
teaching managers and supervisors how to improve loyalty and
productivity with recognition, and offering programs that range
from preventing job burnout to minimizing workplace conflict. A
frequent keynote speaker and active member of the National
Speakers Association, she addresses audiences on issues ranging
from motivating volunteers to retaining the best employees and
keeping them happy and productive.

Cindy grew up in the San Francisco Bay Area and later graduated with a BA from the education department of San Jose State
University. She now lives in Santa Cruz, California, with her husband, Gary. Her son, Tony, is a recent college graduate. Cindy uses

the recognition techniques presented in *Make Their Day!* in nearly every aspect of her life: from parenting to marriage to work relationships and even her relationship with her mechanic!

For information about services and programs, you can contact:

CINDY VENTRICE
Potential Unlimited
PO Box 3437
Santa Cruz, CA 95063
Phone: 831–476–4224
E-mail:cventrice@potential-unltd.com
Web site: www.maketheirday.com.

Please see next pages for other books
from Berrett-Koehler Publishers

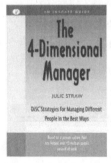